Library Technolo...
R E P O R T S
Expert Guides to Library Systems and Services

Improving Access to and Delivery of Academic Content from Libraries

Aaron Tay

ALA TechSource
American Library Association

Library Technology
R E P O R T S

ALA TechSource purchases fund advocacy, awareness, and accreditation programs for library professionals worldwide.

Volume 58, Number 6

Improving Access to and Delivery of Academic
Content from Libraries
ISBN: 978-0-8389-3813-3
DOI: https://doi.org/10.5860/ltr.58n6

American Library Association

225 N. Michigan Ave., Suite 1300
Chicago, IL 60601-7616 USA
alatechsource.org
800-545-2433, ext. 4299
312-944-6780
312-280-5275 (fax)

Editor

Samantha Kundert

Copy Editor

Judith Lauber

Production

ALA Production Services

Cover Design

Alejandra Diaz and ALA Production Services

Library Technology Reports (ISSN 0024-2586) is published eight times a year (January, March, April, June, July, September, October, and December) by American Library Association, 225 N. Michigan Ave., Suite 1300, Chicago, IL 60601-7616. It is managed by ALA TechSource, a unit of the publishing department of ALA. Periodical postage paid at Chicago, Illinois, and at additional mailing offices. POSTMASTER: Send address changes to Library Technology Reports, 225 N. Michigan Ave., Suite 1300, Chicago, IL 60601-7616.

ALA TechSource

About the Author

Aaron Tay is Lead, Data Services, at Singapore Management University Libraries. An academic librarian with over fifteen years of experience, he has served in two academic libraries in Singapore in a variety of functions, including reference, cataloging, liaison, and analytics. He has interests in library discovery, bibliometrics, analytics, and more.

He has been blogging his thoughts on librarianship at the award-winning blog *Aaron Tay's Musings about Librarianship*—https://musingsaboutlibrarianship .blogspot.com—since 2009 and tweets at @aarontay.

Abstract

While academic libraries have traditionally focused on discovery, helping users to seamlessly access resources available behind a paywall is becoming equally important. The emergence of Sci-Hub into the public eye has led not only to more academic piracy but also to the discovery that academic users were using Sci-Hub for the sheer convenience of not needing to authenticate. This and other reasons have led to the suspicion that there is a need to improve and streamline the processes for users to authenticate and access resources available behind paywalls.

While the traditional solutions are IP authentication and federated access, we now have a slew of possible alternatives or improvements. These include initiatives like SeamlessAccess and GetFTR as well as the emergence of new third-party tools known as access broker browser extensions, such as Lean Library and LibKey Nomad.

Google has also been working toward a solution dubbed Campus Activated Subscriber Access (CASA), while the rise of content syndication partnerships between publishers like Springer Nature and ResearchGate gives the possibility of authentication using researcher profiles.

This issue of *Library Technology Reports*, "Improving Access to and Delivery of Academic Content from Libraries," will walk the interested nontechnical librarian through understanding the fundamentals needed to plan for these new developments.

Contents

Contents, continued

Chapter 1

The Access and Delivery Problem for Libraries

Introduction

The problem of discovery has been a long-standing area of study for academic libraries. In the online era, we transitioned from abstracts and indexing subject databases to full-text databases. This was followed by the attempt to aggregate access to all the disparate e-resources in one centralized platform. To that end, we went from federated search engines to web-scale discovery engines in the 2010s, and the promise of semantic linked data now beckons as we struggle to define our online services in comparison to Google.

However, as interesting as discovery is to academic libraries, it tells only part of the story. While discovery—the process of helping users find what is potentially useful to them—is important, access and delivery are equally important. The access and delivery process allows users to easily check if they have access to the content that they are interested in and to quickly access the content. If a user does not have access, they should be supplied with useful options such as getting access via document delivery.

In the online environment, these are some typical scenarios that users face:

- *Scenario A:* A faculty member googles an article and lands on a JSTOR journal article landing page. Because they are off campus, JSTOR is unable to determine that they have institutional access, and they get a paywall. How does the faculty member authenticate and access the full text?
- *Scenario B:* Same scenario as above, except this time the link leads to an article on a journal provider's platform that the subscriptions of the faculty member's institution do not cover, though the same article can be accessed on another platform. How does the faculty member know this?
- *Scenario C:* A postgraduate finds a paper of interest by searching on the Mendeley online platform. How do they know whether they have access to the full text through their institution?

While I have used access to a journal article as examples of content the user wants to access, similar scenarios apply for users trying to access e-books, databases, and other resources licensed online by the library. The fact that today's online context involves the user moving between multiple devices (e.g., desktop, mobile phone, tablet) further complicates matters.

In all three scenarios, if the users are off campus, it may not be obvious to them how they can access the content or even determine if they have access to it. Alternatively, they may be given options that result in broken links, which may mean inaccurate metadata was supplied. While this report focuses on newer authentication workflows, many of these methods ultimately rely on the accuracy of metadata that is shared throughout the supply chain. This report will briefly mention some of the issues related to inaccuracy of metadata and how some systems, like GetFTR, try to improve on traditional methods. I recommend referring to other texts on the topic such as Pacific University Press's Managing Licensed E-Resources web page for more guidance on the issue.

> *Managing Licensed E-Resources*
> http://www.lib.pacificu.edu/create/pup/pacific
> -university-press-all-books/pup-managing-licensed
> -eresources/

In the online environment, solving such issues typically falls under access management, and understanding the concepts of authentication and authorization will be helpful. We will cover that topic in the next chapter. However, for now, let us consider why it is worthwhile to spend effort studying and understanding the access and delivery issue.

Why Care about the Access and Delivery Issue?

- While discovery is getting less important, delivery and access are becoming steadily more important for academic libraries.
- Delivery and access library solutions need to be more seamless to increase patron awareness of library resources.
- Libraries need to be aware of what new alternatives are available to help solve the problems of access and delivery.
- Publishers are affected by competitors such as Sci-Hub and the fear of leakage.

While Discovery Is Getting Less Important, Delivery and Access Are Becoming Steadily More Important for Academic Libraries

In the mid-2000s, Lorcan Dempsey coined and popularized the phrase "Discovery happens elsewhere" and a few years later introduced the idea of library services, particularly discovery services, moving to the network level, which he dubbed "web-scale."[1] Both trends collectively foreshadowed the decline in the prominence of library discovery services and the rising popularity and importance of large web-scale gateway services such as Google, Google Scholar, and ResearchGate. Since then, various surveys of researchers have confirmed the rising importance of academic search engines and academic social networking sites and the declining importance of library discovery services.[2]

One of the first academic libraries to take this seriously was Utrecht University, which argued provocatively in a series of talks that it was time to start "thinking the unthinkable" and even consider "doing away with the library catalogue." Simone Kortekaas and Bianca Kramer of Utrecht University argued back in 2014

> At Utrecht University we strongly believe that academic libraries have lost their role in the discovery of scientific information and should focus on delivery instead. . . . We have to admit that others can do a better job on discovery, so don't spend too much time on this. Make a priority of your delivery task and rethink the way you can provide value for your users.[3]

As a result, Utrecht University closed down its custom-made discovery tool, Omega, and did not replace it with then-trendy web-scale discovery services (EBSCO Discovery Service, Summon, Primo, etc.) that most academic libraries were implementing or already had in place. Instead, it focused on supporting delivery of items for users who were using Google Scholar and OCLC's WorldCat. It also developed a simple JavaScript bookmarklet for users and a Chrome browser extension called UU Easy Access, both of which helped users gain access when they were on a page without needing to go back to the library home page. The browser extension, developed by a staff member at Utrecht University, was later spun off to become Lean Library, one of the leading access broker browser extensions, which we will feature in chapter 3.[4] While Utrecht's approach was not very popular, one does not need to take an extreme position on discovery to recognize that focusing on improving delivery may also be a good idea. (This is not to say libraries should totally ignore the discovery issue. Academic libraries increasingly have to engage in activities to promote content from their community, such as to enhance the discovery of content deposited into institutional repositories.)

WorldCat
https://www.worldcat.org

Lean Library
https://www.leanlibrary.com

Delivery and Access Library Solutions Are Not Seamless Enough

Whether or not you accept the idea that the role of library discovery is diminishing, is there any reason our delivery and access options need improving? In a 2015 analysis that was influential, at least in the publisher world, titled *Meeting Researchers Where They Start: Streamlining Access to Scholarly Resources*, Roger C. Schonfeld of Ithaka S+R systematically detailed the problems researchers face when trying to access library resources.[5] Some of the issues he identified were

- access solutions being overreliant on users starting at the library websites or doing research only on campus
- overly complicated, unintuitive workflows as well as inconsistent, confusing labeling for proxy solutions and federated SAML solutions such as Shibboleth
- access and delivery solutions that are often not optimized for mobile devices or multiple devices
- unstable and unreliable linking mechanisms

Table 1.1. Some current fundamental issues with library delivery and proposed solutions

Need	Traditional solution	Weaknesses	Emerging solution
User lands on a content owner site and tries to access the content. Site needs to authenticate user.	IP and proxy solution	• Unintuitive to use when off campus and when not starting at library home page	• Access broker browser extensions (chapter 3) • Campus Activated Subscriber Access (CASA; chapter 5) • Content syndication with ResearchGate (chapter 5)
	Federated access	• Nonstandard and unintuitive log-in screen	• SeamlessAccess (chapter 4)
User lands on a discovery platform site and tries to check if they have access anywhere. Site needs to determine where to send the user where they may have access (including free-to-read copies).	Library link resolver (typically OpenURL)	• Poor link reliability (various reasons) • Generated links not automatically leading to full text	• GetFTR (chapter 4) • LibKey infrastructure (chapter 3) • Access broker browser extensions (chapter 3)
User needs to access resources on multiple devices, including mobile devices.	None		• Campus Activated Subscriber Access (CASA) validation shared across all devices with the same Google account (chapter 5)

Most of these issues are probably not news to librarians, who often need to help users with e-resource troubleshooting. In particular, some of these problems—such as the inadequacy of IP authentication with proxy-based solutions and the unreliability of library linking solutions, particularly OpenURL—had been well known for over a decade,[6] although the issue with mobile devices was relatively new.

Still, Schonfeld's analysis was one of the first by a nonlibrarian to bring it all together. Promoted further by Schonfeld, a relatively prominent member of the publisher community, in talks as well as on the popular blog *Scholarly Kitchen*,[7] it got a lot of attention among librarians and also caught the interest of publishers and researchers active in scholarly communication circles. We will consider a deeper analysis of some of these problems in the next chapter, but for a brief summary of issues and some possible solutions, refer to table 1.1.

Availability of New Alternatives to Solve the Problems of Access and Delivery

Even if we admit that the library access and delivery process has room for improvement, are solutions available? Indeed, since the mid-2010s, a whole slew of tools and technologies have started to emerge that either try to improve on existing technologies—IP authentication and proxy solutions, federated access solutions—or introduce new methods for access and delivery. Some of these solutions, which will be covered in future chapters, are

- library access broker browser extensions—chapter 3
- federated access solutions—SeamlessAccess and GetFTR—chapter 4

- Google's Campus Activated Subscriber Access (CASA), content syndication partnership between Springer Nature and ResearchGate—chapter 5

While these solutions may not handle every issue identified by Schonfeld's analysis, they do mostly address the meat of the issue, which is to help provide more seamless access to content.

Competitors Such as Sci-Hub and the Fear of Leakage

While some of the solutions mentioned above are journal-publisher-independent approaches, many publishers are now supporting federated identity approaches to access via the SeamlessAccess coalition, which was the successor organization to 2016's RA21, as well as the GetFTR initiative in 2019. The SeamlessAccess coalition also seeks to eventually eliminate IP-based authentication methods of access.[8] Why this sudden interest by publishers in improving the delivery process?

> *SeamlessAccess Coalition*
> https://www.seamlessaccess.org
>
> *GetFTR*
> https://www.getfulltextresearch.com

While we can speculate on why publishers decided on such a move, one reason is probably competition from Sci-Hub. Sci-Hub, a website that illegally provides free access to academic content, first rose to prominence in 2015 and 2016, when big publishers such as Elsevier brought lawsuits against it. While a certain amount of piracy was expected, an analysis of Sci-Hub logs from September 2015 through February 2016 led to the surprising finding that many of its users were academic users who probably already had legal access via their institutions.[9]

Similarly, an analysis by Bianca Kramer of Utrecht University, using the same logs, attempted to answer a similar question: "Do people use Sci-Hub to get papers they do not otherwise have access to, or do they (also) go to Sci-Hub for convenience: a one-stop shop to get access, without having to navigate library and publisher websites?"[10] By restricting analysis to entries in the Sci-Hub log that correspond to the IP addresses from the university, Kramer found that over 60 percent of Sci-Hub accesses were to content that could be downloaded via library subscriptions and inferred that many users were using Sci-Hub for convenience rather than access.[11] If this surprising finding is typical, it suggests that library access and delivery options are perhaps often too unintuitive for many researchers so that the researchers prefer to use Sci-Hub rather than jumping through library access and authentication hoops to gain access to what they want.

So why do these findings bother publishers? Since the value of big deals that libraries sign with publishers reflects the usage reports (typically downloads from COUNTER reports) generated by publisher platforms, any usage that happens off the platform on sites like Sci-Hub would lower the value of the deal and would be considered what Roger Schonfeld called publisher "leakage."[12] Recent surveys of readers revealed that

> If you compare the data which shows that 80% of people are viewing the version of record with the data that shows only around 45–50% of article downloads come from the publisher web site, we can conclude that a significant proportion of Version of Record articles are being obtained from resources outside of publisher control.[13]

To be fair, if leakage is defined as any usage that happens off the publisher platform, it would include downloads by users from both legitimate sources such as SSRN and institutional repositories and illegal sites like Sci-Hub. As we shall see in chapter 4, publisher-supported initiatives like SeamlessAccess and GetFTR help plug this leakage by providing more seamless access to downloads available via publisher platforms.[14]

Does Open Access Make the Access and Discovery Question Moot?

The open-access (OA) penetration rate has been steadily rising, and for the publication year 2020, over 50 percent of publications tracked by Digital Science's Dimensions product were found for the first time to be OA.[15] (As of December 2021, Dimensions tracks over 100 million articles.) A conservative projection is that by 2025, 70 percent of all article views will be of OA articles.[16] With developments like Plan S in the wings, it seems likely that the momentum toward OA will continue. Does this mean that focusing on access and delivery is likely to be wasted effort since in a soon-to-be OA world, access and delivery problems will automatically solve themselves? Not necessarily.

First, such projections tend to use a broad definition of OA and usually include both version of record (VoR) and accepted manuscript, if not even earlier versions. Authors are known to have clear preference for VoR, so this is not a trivial distinction. If we achieve high levels of OA in the near future, but a big part of this OA is achieved via non-VoR, there is still a place for access and delivery mechanisms to guide the user to VoR copies.

Second, as it currently stands, when we talk about OA, we are talking mostly about journal articles and to a much lesser extent about books. However, the library provides access to paywalled e-resources that go beyond journal articles and books. For example, the library provides access to A&I databases, financial and business databases, and image databases, all of which will continue to require good access and delivery mechanics for our users.

Last, the rising availability of OA copies of various versions of resources also means that the library can play a role in guiding users to help them discover and access OA copies when they are stumped by a paywall that cannot be bypassed by library subscriptions.

Conclusion

In this chapter, we started by distinguishing the problem for academic libraries of supporting discovery from that of supporting access and delivery. We asserted that delivery and access are an important area of library service to focus on and provided four reasons for that assertion. Chief among the reasons was the less-than-intuitive nature of our current access and delivery systems, which may have led some of our readers to prefer to use Sci-Hub, which does not have any authentication system. We also briefly mentioned the major different tools and solutions available to libraries and ended with a section explaining why even with the rise of OA, libraries should still focus on delivery and access.

In the next chapter, we will explain the basic concepts of authentication and authorization for library e-resources.

Notes

1. Lorcan Dempsey, "Discovery Happens Elsewhere," *LorcanDempsey.Net* (blog), September 16, 2007, https://www.lorcandempsey.net/orweblog/discovery-happens-elsewhere/; Lorcan Dempsey, "Thirteen Ways of Looking at Libraries, Discovery, and the Catalog: Scale, Workflow, Attention," *Educause Review*, December 10, 2012, https://er.educause.edu/articles/2012/12/thirteen-ways-of-looking-at-libraries-discovery-and-the-catalog-scale-workflow-attention.
2. Tracy Gardner and Simon Inger, *How Readers Discover Content in Scholarly Publications: Trends in Reader Behaviour from 2005 to 2021* (Renew Consultants, July 2021), https://renewconsultants.com/wp-content/uploads/2021/07/How-Readers-Discover-Content-2021.pdf.
3. Simone Kortekaas and Bianca Kramer, "Thinking the Unthinkable: Doing Away with the Library Catalogue," *Insights* 27, no. 3 (November 3, 2014): 244, https://doi.org/10.1629/2048-7754.174.
4. Johan Tiistra, "Lean Library's Browser Extension: Seamless Delivery for Users," guest post, *Aaron Tay's Musings about Librarianship* (blog), May 30, 2017, https://musingsaboutlibrarianship.blogspot.com/2017/05/guest-post-lean-librarys-browser.html.
5. Roger C. Schonfeld, *Meeting Researchers Where They Start: Streamlining Access to Scholarly Resources*, issue brief (New York: Ithaka S+R, March 26, 2015), https://sr.ithaka.org/publications/meeting-researchers-where-they-start-streamlining-access-to-scholarly-resources/.
6. Cindi Trainor and Jason Price, *Rethinking Library Linking: Breathing New Life into OpenURL* (Chicago: American Library Association, 2010).
7. Roger C. Schonfeld, "Dismantling the Stumbling Blocks That Impede Researcher Access to E-Resources," *Scholarly Kitchen* (blog), November 13, 2015, https://scholarlykitchen.sspnet.org/2015/11/13/dismantling-the-stumbling-blocks-that-impede-researcher-access-to-e-resources/.
8. Todd A. Carpenter, Heather Flanagan, and Chris Shillum, "Myth Busting: Five Commonly Held Misconceptions about RA21 (and One Rumor Confirmed)," *Scholarly Kitchen* (blog), February 7, 2018, https://scholarlykitchen.sspnet.org/2018/02/07/myth-busting-five-commonly-held-misconceptions-ra21/.
9. John Bohannon, "Who's Downloading Pirated Papers? Everyone," *Science* 352, no. 6285 (April 25, 2016): 508–12, https://doi.org/10.1126/science.352.6285.508.
10. Bianca Kramer, "Sci-Hub: Access or Convenience? A Utrecht Case Study (Part 1)," *Library Blog*, Utrecht University, June 20, 2016, https://ubublog.sites.uu.nl/2016/06/20/sci-hub-utrecht-case-study-part-1/.
11. Bianca Kramer, "Sci-Hub: Access or Convenience? A Utrecht Case Study (Part 2)," *I&M/I&O 2.0* (blog), June 20, 2016, https://im2punt0.wordpress.com/2016/06/20/sci-hub-access-or-convenience-a-utrecht-case-study-part-2/.
12. Roger C. Schonfeld, "Is the Value of the Big Deal in Decline?," *Scholarly Kitchen* (blog), March 7, 2019, https://scholarlykitchen.sspnet.org/2019/03/07/value-big-deal-leakage/.
13. Gardner and Inger, *How Readers Discover Content*, 32.
14. Roger C. Schonfeld, "Publishers Announce a Major New Service to Plug Leakage," *Scholarly Kitchen* (blog), December 3, 2019, https://scholarlykitchen.sspnet.org/2019/12/03/publishers-announce-plug-leakage/.
15. Daniel Hook, "Open Access Surpasses Subscription Publication Globally for the First Time," *Dimensions* (blog), February 24, 2021, https://www.dimensions.ai/blog/open-access-surpasses-subscription-publication-globally-for-the-first-time/.
16. Heather Piwowar, Jason Priem, and Richard Orr, "The Future of OA: A Large-Scale Analysis Projecting Open Access Publication and Readership," preprint, bioRxiv, October 9, 2019, 795310, https://doi.org/10.1101/795310.

Chapter 2

Authentication, Authorization, and the Appropriate Copy Problem

Some Basic Concepts for Access Management of Library Resources

B efore we start to discuss problems and solutions for access to library resources, it is useful to know some basic concepts regarding authentication and authorization for access management.

The issue that authentication and authorization attempt to solve boils down to the following question: When a user lands on a content owner's platform, such as a journal platform, should the content owner allow the user to access paywalled content?

Another related problem common to delivery of library resources, particularly for journal articles, is the "appropriate copy problem."[1] The appropriate copy problem arises from the fact that content such as journal articles can reside in multiple locations online. For example, a journal article can be available at a publisher site (such as Wiley), an aggregator or a reseller site (such as EBSCOhost platform), and open-access repositories (such as institutional repositories), and the most appropriate copy varies depending on the entitlements of the user making the request. (For example, what institution do they belong to, and given their position, what are they allowed to access?) This issue comes up particularly for discovery systems such as Google Scholar and citation indexes, which do not carry the full-text content.[2] Because these are the first point of reference that many students look to when researching online, these researchers may not know that they would have full-text access through their library's database. As a result, answering the appropriate copy problem here involves determining where to direct users to get the most suitable copy. See figure 2.1 for example scenarios of these issues.

In this chapter, we will focus on the fundamental concepts necessary for understanding authentication issues and the solutions that traditionally have been used to answer them. We'll also look at some common problems that occur with these traditional solutions.

Authentication and Authorization

Understanding how access management works can be technical; however, a very good resource targeted at librarians exists—Kristina Botyriute's *Access to Online Resources: A Guide for the Modern Librarian* provides the essentials needed for a library worker to quickly get up to speed with the issues.[3] I encourage you to refer to that source for more detail.

From a technical point of view, when someone logs in to access a resource, they go through two distinct but related processes:

1. The process of *authentication* confirms that users are who they say they are.
2. Once users are authenticated, the process of *authorization* ensures users are given the right permissions to access resources.

Take this simple example: an undergraduate student from the school of social science may log in to your system with a username and password. After the system authenticates the student, it looks up what access rights they have and grants those rights to them. This is the process of *authorization*.

Improving Access to and Delivery of Academic Content from Libraries   **Aaron Tay**

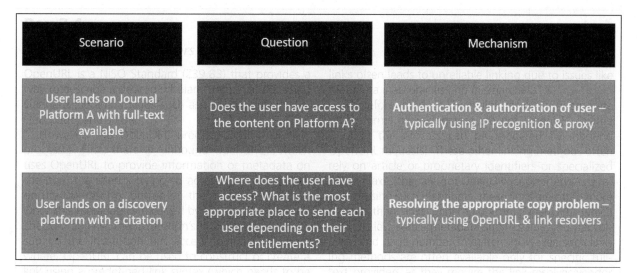

Scenario	Question	Mechanism
User lands on Journal Platform A with full-text available	Does the user have access to the content on Platform A?	Authentication & authorization of user – typically using IP recognition & proxy
User lands on a discovery platform with a citation	Where does the user have access? What is the most appropriate place to send each user depending on their entitlements?	Resolving the appropriate copy problem – typically using OpenURL & link resolvers

Figure 2.1
Two common delivery issues for library resources—authentication and authorization, and the appropriate copy problem.

While the two processes are related, they are distinct. For example, a user trying to log in to the JSTOR database to access a journal article can be successfully authenticated as a current student at Institution X (we will discuss how later), but they may not be authorized to access that particular article in JSTOR. Similarly, two users from the same institution but different departments may have different access rights. For example, a medical researcher might have access to Embase, a specialized medical database, that another researcher from a different department in the same institution might not have. In the next section, we will discuss the three major ways academic libraries provide authentication and authorization today: (1) individual account passwords, (2) IP recognition, and (3) SAML-based SSO methods.

Providing Access with Individual Usernames and Passwords

Imagine a scenario where you are the electronic resource librarian at an institution that has successfully negotiated a subscription with access to a bundle of journal titles on the JSTOR platform. Great! Now, how does the publisher ensure that only authorized people (users from your institution) are allowed access to the full-text articles in these journals on JSTOR? One obvious but very uncommon way (particularly in this scenario) is to issue individual usernames and passwords to everyone. Each user enters their own username and password to authenticate themselves and access the resource. From the user's point of view, registering and remembering a separate set of user credentials for each library resource is inconvenient. For many students, any access barrier is likely to push them into the arms of free web services and content. Another issue is how to handle turnover when users

Box 2.1

Rarely Used Work-Arounds for Passwords

One attempt to work around the problem with passwords is to provide a single shared username and password for all members of your institution. Typically, this works by making users of your institution sign in and authenticate themselves first on a web page before displaying the username and password they can use directly on the resource.

The problem with this solution is that it is not very user-friendly because the user needs to authenticate twice (once with the institution and once with the publisher) to gain access. In addition, there might be concerns on whether the account will be shared with unauthorized users. It is difficult to track who is actually using the account if there is a need for this information. Still, this might be the only solution for publishers that do not support IP authentication methods.

There have been other work-arounds, such as making users log in to virtual environments or embedding passwords and tokens in EZproxy sign-ins, but such work-arounds are quite frail and can easily break.

join and leave your institution. Surely the publishers expect you to ensure that only current students and staff have access, which requires quite a bit of maintenance. Now multiply this effort by the number of resources you subscribe to. Clearly, doing this manually is not sustainable except for a small select number of resources with low usage.

For some other work-arounds to address these issues, see box 2.1.

In this example, JSTOR is a popular database highly used by students and researchers. Therefore, manually maintaining individual accounts and passwords is

Library Technology Reports alatechsource.org August/September 2022

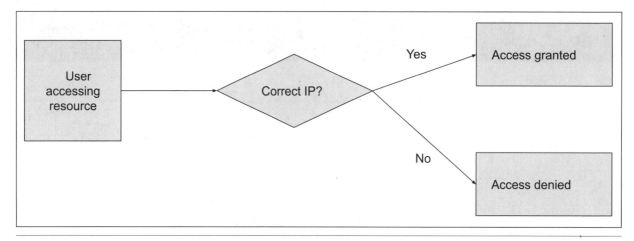

Figure 2.2
Accessing library resources via IP authentication (correct IP vs. wrong IP)

most certainly not viable. In fact, academic libraries seldom provide access by individual usernames and passwords because the effort is too great. Instead, IP recognition is far more commonly used today.

Providing Access through IP Recognition

As we have seen, issuing individual passwords is not sustainable. Thankfully, this is not the main way institutions provide access for users to most of their resources. Today, access to most online resources subscribed to by libraries is provided via IP recognition. The idea is simple. When electronic resource librarians subscribe to an online resource, all they need to do is provide a list of IP addresses (the IP range) that are used by users of your community to access the resources. Typically, this would be the IP range of your users when they are on campus using the campus Wi-Fi. The publisher of the resource will set up its server to allow access whenever it receives a request coming from these IP addresses. Put in another way, we create a whitelist of IP addresses where requesters from those IPs are allowed access (see figure 2.2).

From the users' point of view, access is seamless because they do not need to do anything, not even explicitly sign in, as long as they are on campus and in the campus Wi-Fi range. Arguably, access might be *too seamless*, as users may not even know that they are accessing the institution's subscriptions if they miss the sometimes-subtle signs on the publisher platforms that recognize them via IP.

THE OFF-CAMPUS PROBLEM: IP RECOGNITION AND PROXY SERVERS

So far, we have seen that when libraries use IP recognition to provide access, users get a very seamless experience as long as they are requesting the resource via the right IP address (i.e., they are on campus

using campus Wi-Fi). However, in our global and post-COVID-19 world, expecting our users to access resources only on campus seems unrealistic. So how do we provide access with IP recognition when users are off campus? There are two main methods: (1) proxy servers and (2) VPNs. Both methods make the user's request appear to be from the right IP address, but proxy methods are far more popular today, so let us discuss them.

A proxy server, in simplified terms, is a piece of software that sits between you, the user, and the online resource you are trying to access; it sends and retrieves content on your behalf. Today, the most popular proxy server used for this purpose in libraries is OCLC's EZproxy, but others exist. Let's see how this works. Again, let us take the example of a user trying to access a journal that is available only behind a paywall. If the user is off campus and tries to directly access the resource, they will be denied access because their IP address is not recognized (see figure 2.3).

One way around the problem is through a proxy server, which requests the resource on behalf of the user and retrieves the content on their behalf (see figure 2.4).

But how does the user get the proxy server to make the request on their behalf? They will need to use a specially treated link to do so—one that is set up to direct user requests through the proxy. This type of link is informally called a *proxied link*. Here is an example of such a proxied link from my institution. This link, when clicked, directs the user's request to access the JSTOR database (in bold type: http://www.jstor.org) via the proxy server.

> http://libproxy.smu.edu.sg/login?url=http://lib proxy.smu.edu.sg/login?url=**http://www.jstor.org**[4]

But how does the user find such a link? One way is for the user to go to the library home page, look for

Library Technology Reports   alatechsource.org   August/September 2022

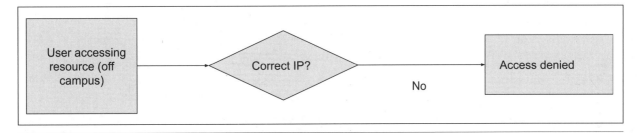

Figure 2.3
Prevented from accessing library resources when off campus

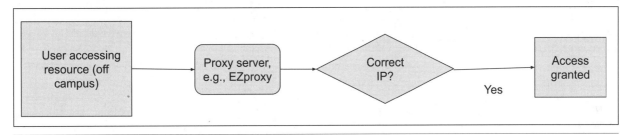

Figure 2.4
Granted access via proxy when accessing library resources off campus

the desired online resource (e.g., via the library search engine or database A–Z list), and click on the link provided; access is granted. How do we then ensure that unauthorized users cannot use this method by using the previous link? Simple: whenever someone tries to access a resource via the proxy server, they will need to authenticate themselves with a sign-on.

Assuming the proxy server configuration is set correctly for each online resource that the library is licensed to access, users need only to use the same sign-on (which typically is their institutional sign-on credentials) each time regardless of the online resource they are trying to access via the proxy. For more details on proxy servers and configuration settings for libraries, please refer to the documentation of the proxy server you are using.

Overall, despite any drawbacks of this method (see discussion in the next section), IP recognition is currently the dominant way access is provided. For a typical library, access to 70 to 80 percent of resources will be provided this way, though SAML-based methods may be rising in popularity.

Single Sign-On with SAML

As noted in chapter 1, in the section Delivery and Access Library Solutions Are Not Seamless Enough, one of the current major situations that cause access to be less seamless is when users are off campus. To benefit from IP authentication and proxy solutions when off campus, they will need to start from library-controlled pages with proxied links.

Unfortunately, we know that most of our users do not start their research from our library home pages. Assuming they are off campus when they land on a resource, they will not be able to benefit from IP recognition, nor use the proxy, unless they have installed a software solution, such as an access broker browser extension like Lean Library, that helps them with access (see chapter 3).

However, some of these web pages have a log-in button or even a Log in with Your Institution button, and some users are able to obtain access through that method. Other times they may see strange jargon like "Log in with Shibboleth" or "Sign in with OpenAthens" and try to log in with those (see figure 2.5).

Both Shibboleth and OpenAthens employ SAML (Security Assertion Markup Language) technology. At their best, such solutions will be intuitive and user-friendly enough that users can easily select their institution (a process known as Where-Are-You-From, or WAYF, which will we discuss further in chapter 4) and then sign in immediately with their existing university user credentials without the need to create new accounts and passwords. The experience is akin to options like "Sign in with Google" or "Sign in with Facebook" that you may have used to sign on to other platforms, except that instead of using your social network credential account, you use your institutional account.[5] This type of sign-in process is known as *single sign-on* (SSO) and can be implemented in a few ways. In the academic library space, SAML-based technologies are usually employed and are the major alternative to IP recognition.

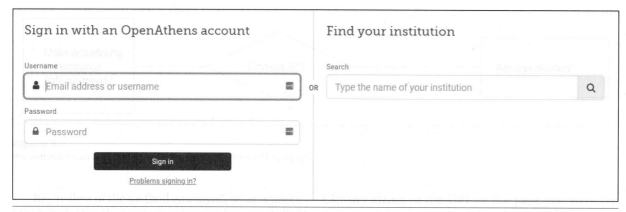

Figure 2.5
Example of SAML sign-in options

SAML IN DEPTH

SAML is an open standard used for identity management by allowing different parties to exchange authentication and authorization data. The standard, which was first created in 2003 and was updated to 2.0 in 2005, underlies both Shibboleth and OpenAthens logins, which are commonly used in the academic library space.

See box 2.2 for information on differences between Shibboleth and OpenAthens.

SAML SSO methods improve on simple account password systems in two ways: (1) the user does not need to register and create user accounts in advance, and (2) the user does not need to create and remember new usernames and passwords for each SAML-enabled service. Instead, they may just need to use the institutional credentials that they have no doubt memorized by using them for accessing common university services, such as e-mail, university Wi-Fi, and so on. At worse, they may just need to remember one more common password for access to all library electronic resources. All access is controlled centrally, so access to all these services, including SAML-enabled services, can be revoked when the user leaves the institution.

So how does this work under the hood? Whenever a user tries to log in via Shibboleth- or OpenAthens-enabled resource, they select the institution they claim to be from. The service, which is termed a *service provider* (SP) in SAML speak, doesn't take this at face value but redirects the user back to an identity provider (IdP) to verify that they really are from the institution selected. The IdP may then verify the user. Typically, the user might sign in with their institutional password, and once the user is verified, the IdP will redirect them back to the original SP and assert that the user is indeed verified as being from the institution they claim to be from. The SP will use this information to provide access (see figure 2.6).

For example, a user clicks to sign in to JSTOR via OpenAthens and indicates they are from your

Box 2.2

What Is the Difference between Shibboleth and OpenAthens?

Both Shibboleth and OpenAthens support SSO infrastructure via SAML.

Shibboleth is open-source software and can be difficult to install and manage for libraries with little experience. A typical library would need to work with the institution's campus IT department to setup Shibboleth use for library resources. Using OpenAthens is less complex than using Shibboleth because it is a cloud-based solution for libraries looking to go down the SAML route. Among other advantages, OpenAthens provides easy-to-use analytics and support (governed by a service level agreement) for setting up access to different resources, troubleshooting, and more. It is essentially an easy way for libraries with no expertise in SAML to set up an identity server.

For more information on OpenAthens, refer to its website, https://www.openathens.net.

institution. JSTOR, which is the SP, redirects the user to your university's IdP, which is usually a server where you sign on to access various university-related services such as e-mail. The user then signs in as normal, and if authentication is successful, the IdP will redirect the user back to the SP (JSTOR) with an assertion confirming that the user is indeed from your institution.

In chapter 4, we will discuss in more detail what assertions are eligible to be sent back to the SP, but for now let's just say that the IdP asserts to the SP that that user is a valid user from your institution. The SP can now be sure that the user is a valid member of your institution and can provide the appropriate level of rights (authorization). If most library resources are enabled to support SAML in the same way, this means all the user needs to remember is one set of account

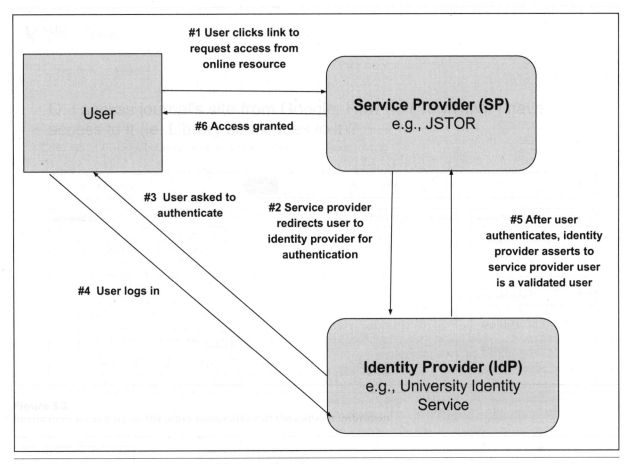

Figure 2.6
Diagram of the SAML SSO process

passwords to access all the services provided by their institution, from e-mail and Wi-Fi to learning management resource, library account, and, yes, online resources like databases.

SAML AND FEDERATION

In the previous section, we've seen the following steps:

1. A user tries to sign in to access a resource from an SP by indicating which institution they are from.
2. The SP redirects the user to the appropriate IdP based on their selected institution.
3. The user signs in with the IdP.
4. The IdP checks whether the sign-in is correct and then redirects the user back to the SP with a trusted assertation that the user is verified.
5. The SP grants access.

But how does the SP at step 2 know the location of the appropriate IdP? The simplest answer is that the SP and the IdP have an agreement in advance, and, in practice, this type of one-to-one relationship is often employed. In a scenario where there is only one SP

and one IdP, knowing to which IdP to send users is a simple matter. However, a service like JSTOR may have thousands of customers from all around the world, so maintaining lists of customers and their IdPs can get unwieldy. Similarly, the library and the institution may want to enable SAML with hundreds, if not thousands, of services. It is important to note that SAML can be used to authenticate all sorts of online resources, not just library resources.

This is where the idea of *federations* comes into play. Rather than SPs contracting directly with individual institutions and IdPs, they join federations or more precisely identity federations. SPs also joining those same identity federations results in data and standards that can be trusted by both sides without the need for individual arrangements. At a very basic level, identity federations are trusted registries where SPs and IdPs can do lookups to find metadata of institutions and organizations as well as agreed-on protocols for completing the SAML process. There are dozens of identity federations out there, including the following:

- UK Access Management Federation for Education and Research

- InCommon
- Australian Access Federation (AAF)

They are often at the national level, but global ones like OpenAthens do exist.

IS SAML A PERFECT SOLUTION?

So far, SAML SSO, with its promise of single sign-on even when the user is off campus, seems to be a better solution than IP recognition. To recap, all users have to do on any SAML SSO-supported resource site is

1. Click on the Sign In or Log In button.
2. Sign in with their standard institutional password.

Then access is granted. There is no need to struggle with proxied links or remember unique passwords.

However, there are a couple of issues with this solution. First, not every online resource supports SAML-based authentication. While this is also true for IP authentication, SAML support is still less common, particularly among smaller publishers and content owners. Second, not all libraries have experience with SAML technology, and often expertise on identity federation and identity management resides at the institutional campus IT level. This is particularly true in terms of management of the IdP server. See box 2.3 for information about implementing SAML technology.

Third, depending on how the IdP is set up and the agreements in place, SAML authentication can lead to less privacy for users compared to IP recognition methods. We will discuss this further in chapter 4. Lastly, traditionally, library databases and providers have not been very consistent in the way they signal to users that they support SAML-based authentication. Using jargon like the names OpenAthens and Shibboleth on their web pages, coupled with poor user interface experiences, tends to lead to poor user experience and low usage rates.

As we will see in chapter 4, a sign-in process where you select your institution is known as a Where-Are-You-From (WAYF) process. The WAYF process has always been a stumbling block for users. A new initiative, RA21, has risen to tackle this issue by systematically studying the problem and helping to set consistent standards.

The Appropriate Copy Problem Explained

We began this chapter with the scenario of a user landing on an article landing page in the JSTOR database and discussed how JSTOR could authenticate or authorize the user appropriately through their

---

Box 2.3

New to SAML and Federated Access?

Libraries' experience and expertise with SAML varies across regions. Traditionally, UK and to some extent US academic libraries have had the longest experience with such technologies, but not all academic libraries are equally familiar with the technology. For libraries new to SAML technology, considering a switch to this mode of access can be daunting.

Here are some general considerations when thinking of moving in this direction and things to find out. Do you have in-house expertise from people who know and understand the following?

- the basic concepts of service provider (SP), identity provider (IdP), and federated identity
- what attributes are and how they can affect privacy (See chapter 4 for details.)
- what existing identity management servers are used by the larger parent organization
- what identity federations the parent organization and prospective SPs are in

In many institutions, the library itself may have limited experience with SAML access. It may have to consult the larger parent organization, typically the university's central IT unit, which may be managing the IdP, and work closely with it on the possibility of SAML support of library resources.

Alternatively, the library can consider running its own IdP by opting for a service such as OpenAthens.

---

institution and allow the user to gain access to the full text on JSTOR past the paywalls. As discussed earlier, this is not a trivial problem if you want access to be as seamless as possible.

Even if this issue is resolved and the user is authenticated, there are further complications. Thus far, we have assumed that each requested journal article is available in only one location—the location the user is at—and all we need to do is to figure out a way to authenticate the user to determine access past the paywall. However, things can be further complicated if multiple valid copies that are appropriate for different users to access reside at multiple sites rather than just one site.

For example, while a journal article might be available on JSTOR, it might also be available on aggregator sites such as EBSCO or ProQuest or publisher sites such as Wiley. Also, open-access copies might exist in repositories. With all these options, to which copy is it appropriate to send the user?[6] How would a third-party abstract and indexing site such as, say, Web of Science

Library Technology Reports   alatechsource.org   August/September 2022

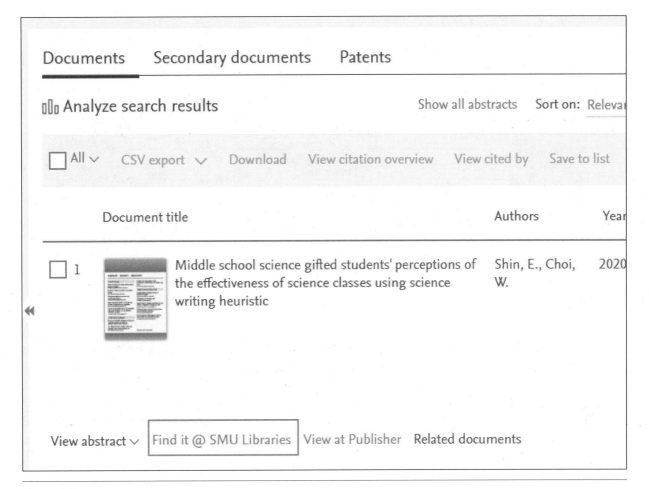

Figure 2.7
Example of a link-resolver button on the SCOPUS platform

or an academic search engine such as Google Scholar know the answer of where to send users?[7] *The appropriate copy problem* was the term coined over twenty years ago to describe this issue. Given an online citation to a journal article, how should systems direct users who have different access and entitlements to the appropriate copy?[8] The solution that libraries and technologists settled upon was the OpenURL standard, which works together with identifiers such as DOIs in library link resolvers to direct users to the appropriate copy.

Today many academic platforms—including popular citation indexes, databases, and academic search engines such as Scopus, Web of Science, Google Scholar, and JSTOR—all support OpenURL and link resolvers, which provide buttons that users can click to be redirected to the appropriate copy wherever that copy may be. See figure 2.7 for an example of such a link-resolver button (in this case labeled Find it @ SMU Libraries) on the Scopus platform. Of course, sometimes no appropriate copy may be available for the user, in which case the typical academic library will display some other service, such as a document delivery service.

OpenURL Briefly Explained

A full discussion of OpenURL is beyond the scope of this text; however, it is useful to be aware of roughly how OpenURL, which is a NISO Standard (Z39.83), works. Let's assume the user has signed on to the platform via either IP authentication or SAML-based methods and the platform knows the user's institution. The idea behind platforms and databases that support OpenURL is that when a user clicks on an OpenURL request link (see figure 2.7), the request link will send information (metadata) about the item the user is requesting back to the user's institutional link resolver. The institution's link resolver will then do the work and figure out where to send the user (see figure 2.8).

More specifically, the OpenURL request typically consists of two parts. The first is the base URL, which contains the address of the user's institutional link server. This base URL may be automatically set when the user authenticates or in some cases may be selected manually by the user (e.g., in Google Scholar). The second part is the OpenURL request itself, which consists of a query, which can be understood as

Library Technology Reports alatechsource.org August/September 2022

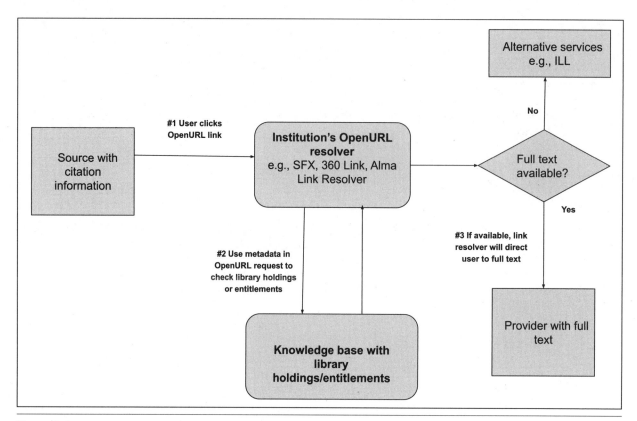

Figure 2.8
Diagram of the process of using an OpenURL link

something that describes information or metadata about the requested resource. This is typically a journal article, but it can be a book, a patent, or any other resource. Here's an example of an OpenURL request for an article in the *Journal of the American Society for Information Science and Technology*:

> https://search.library.smu.edu.sg/discovery
> /openurl?institution=65SMU_INST&vid=65SMU_
> INST:SMU_NUI&volume=59&date=2008&aula
> st=Luyt&issue=2&issn=1532-2882&spage=31
> 8&id=doi:10.1002%2Fasi.20755&auinit=B&tit
> le=Journal%20of%20the%20American%20So
> ciety%20for%20Information%20Science%20
> and%20Technology.&atitle=Improving%20
> Wikipedia%27s%20accuracy:%20Is%20edit%20
> age%20a%20solution%3F&sid=google

The part in bold is the base URL, which sends the user to the right institutional server to check for sources. The remaining part is the metadata describing the requested resource. You may be able to make out from the OpenURL that the requested resource is something that

- is in *Journal of the American Society for Information Science and Technology*
- is in volume 59, issue 2, published in 2008

- has an author with the last name Luyt
- has the article title "Improving Wikipedia's Accuracy: Is Edit Age a Solution?"

The OpenURL standard provides standards on what metadata fields can be used in the OpenURL request: for example, ISSN, volume, issue, starting page, and so on.

Once the user is directed to the appropriate institutional link resolver, the link resolver will use the metadata of the requested item to check the institution's knowledge base (e.g., Alma) to figure out whether the institution has access to that resource and if so try to figure out where to send the user. Using the metadata provided in the OpenURL request, the institutional link resolver will construct a link to the resource. This resolved link could be a link to the publisher, the aggregator, or an open-access copy.

It is important to note that such a process is not magic. For the link resolver to work reliably, the knowledge bases, which contain information on the entitlements of the institution, need to be updated faithfully. Erroneously leaving entitlements out of the knowledge base will lead to the link resolver wrongly indicating something is not available. Doing the opposite will mislead the user into thinking they have access, and they will get an Access Denied message when directed to the requested resource.

Even if the knowledge bases are updated with the right entitlements, links provided via OpenURL might still break. There are many reasons for this, but a common reason is due to errors in the metadata provided in the OpenURL request.[9] For example, the page number or author in an OpenURL request from a platform might be slightly off and thus lead to a wrong link being generated.

It is important to note that, while traditional link resolvers use only OpenURL technology for linking, modern library link resolvers also use other methods to generate links. For more detail, refer to box 2.4.

Is OpenURL a Perfect Solution?

While OpenURL has been a standard in use for over two decades, there have been a variety of problems. Over two decades of research has shown that OpenURL linking tends to be fairly unreliable even for journal articles (which have the highest reliability of all types).[10] There are many reasons for unreliability, such as metadata mismatch inaccuracies, different granularity of linking at the target and source, and the already mentioned inaccuracy of entitlements or holdings data in the knowledge base. In future chapters, we will see how GetFTR and some access broker browser extensions such as LibKey Nomad claim to provide improvements to these issues. More recently, Bulock argued that researchers today work increasingly in open web contexts, which leads them to citations on web pages that either do not support OpenURL or where they are unable to indicate their institutional context.[11] Both access broker browser extensions (covered in chapter 3) and GetFTR (covered in chapter 4) provide some improvements to this problem.

Conclusion

In this chapter, we have presented a high-level view on the issues around providing access via authentication and authorization. We introduced the issues of giving individual accounts to users and outlined two main solutions to these issues: IP recognition and SAML SSO methods.

We also briefly described a further issue with delivery, the appropriate copy problem, and discussed how OpenURL and library link resolvers traditionally handle this problem. In the next chapter, we will discuss access broker browser extensions, which attempt to improve on some of the weaknesses presented here.

Notes

1. Oren Beit-Arie, Miriam Blake, Priscilla Caplan, Dale Flecker, Tim Ingoldsby, Laurence W. Lannom, William H. Mischo, et al., "Linking to the Appropriate Copy: Report of a DOI-Based Prototype," *D-Lib Magazine* 7, no. 9 (September 2001), https://doi.org/10.1045/september2001-caplan.
2. Platforms that attempt to help with the appropriate copy problem are not restricted to discovery systems. Some reference managers, academic social networks, and even some blogs help with this problem by supporting ContextObjects in Spans (COinS). Even

publishers and other platforms that carry content— e.g., JSTOR and EBSCO—also provide alternatives to the user by supporting link resolvers.

3. Kristina Botyriute, *Access to Online Resources: A Guide for the Modern Librarian* (Cham, Switzerland: Springer International Publishing, 2018), https://doi.org/10.1007/978-3-319-73990-8.

4. This is the proxied link for the general JSTOR home page. Specific URLs within JSTOR (e.g., URLs for journal articles) will need to be similarly proxied. In general, once the user is on a proxied URL, all other clicks to links on the same domain will continue to be proxied. It is also important to note that institutions' entitlements may be only a subset of articles on JSTOR and that not all content is fully accessible.

5. Such technologies where you sign in with social accounts like Google or Twitter are usually based on OAuth, which is a different protocol from SAML and differs in some functional ways. For example, while both support SSO, OAuth is a narrower standard that focuses only on authorization, not authentication. Currently, OAuth is not commonly used in the academic space.

6. Here we assume all the different copies are identical; in practice, open-access copies might be different versions of the article—e.g., an accepted manuscript, the version of record, or even a preprint—which further complicates things.

7. While the appropriate copy problem is most salient for discovery platforms and other third-party sites, content platforms such as JSTOR and Wiley do often provide solutions for users who may have access elsewhere.

8. Beit-Arie et al., "Linking to the Appropriate Copy"; Herbert Van de Sompel and Oren Beit-Arie, "Open Linking in the Scholarly Information Environment Using the OpenURL Framework," *D-Lib Magazine* 7, no. 3 (March 2001), https://doi.org/10.1045/march2001-vandesompel.

9. Ex Libris Knowledge Centre, "How Does Incorrect Metadata Break OpenURL Linking," November 1, 2019, https://knowledge.exlibrisgroup.com/Primo/Content_Corner/Primo_Central_Index/Knowledge_Articles/How_does_incorrect_metadata_break_OpenURL_linking.

10. Cindi Trainor and Jason Price, *Rethinking Library Linking: Breathing New Life into OpenURL* (Chicago: American Library Association, 2010).

11. Chris Bulock, "Get Full Text Research and the Search for Appropriate Copies," *Serials Review* 46, no. 2 (2020): 160–62, https://doi.org/10.1080/00987913.2020.1759361.

Chapter 3

Making Access More Seamless with Access Broker Browser Extensions

Introduction

In the previous two chapters, we introduced some of the issues users face when trying to access resources via institutional access; in this chapter, we cover one of the major classes of solutions to this problem—providing access via browser extensions. These browser extensions, which are sometimes called access broker browser extensions, have become very popular in recent years,[1] and most academic libraries officially support them via subscriptions. Some popular examples include Lean Library, LibKey Nomad, EndNote Click (formerly Kopernio), and free alternatives like Google Scholar Button and Lazy Scholar.

Lean Library
https://www.leanlibrary.com

LibKey Nomad
https://thirdiron.com/products/libkey-nomad

EndNote Click
https://click.endnote.com

Lazy Scholar
http://www.lazyscholar.org

The General Concept of Access Broker Browser Extensions

As seen in chapter 2, one of the major barriers to achieving access occurs when the user is off campus and trying to check for access to a resource when not starting on a library-controlled website. Let us use the example from chapter 2 again, where a user tries to access an article directly from JSTOR. Perhaps they are given the direct link in an e-mail or a blog post and as a result, they land on the page, but the system is not able to easily identify who the user is or whether they have the rights to access the article. As we explained in the section Off-Campus Problem: IP Recognition and Proxy Servers in chapter 2, because access to the licensed resource is usually granted via IP recognition and the users are off campus, they will not have the right IP to be granted access (see figure 3.1).

Let us assume for the moment that the user does not use any of the SAML methods, which are covered in chapter 4. In most cases, to get around this problem, the user would need to waste time going back to the library home page to look for the article. Sadly, the user may often give up instead of trying to access it directly through the library web page.

The user experience in this scenario improves greatly and even has a changed outcome when the user has a particular kind of browser extension installed. The improvement happens because the browser extension can easily integrate into their workflow and, with a single click (or even automatically), provide the user access to the full-text article without making the user jump through hoops. The browser extension can accomplish this using a variety of methods in the background: for example, by appending the EZproxy stem to the page the user is on so that access is granted via the proxy or by guiding the user to sign on via SAML methods. The browser extension is not limited to just helping the user gain access to the article on the platform or site, but it can also provide a solution to the appropriate copy problem (see the section Appropriate Copy Problem Explained in chapter 2) by using the metadata of the requested article to direct the user to appropriate copies that may not be on JSTOR.

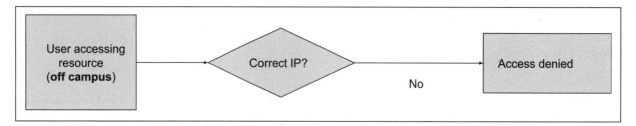

Figure 3.1
Prevented from accessing library resources when off campus

Regardless of the method employed, what is important here is that the browser extension (once installed) is ever-present in the user's browser, providing a convenient point for helping the user gain access.

Proxy Bookmarklets, LibX Toolbars, and Unpaywall: Some Predecessors

The idea of libraries using browser extensions to assist users is not a new idea. During the heyday of Library 2.0 in the early and mid-2000s, librarians experimented with custom toolbars such as conduit toolbars, LibX toolbars, Greasemonkey scripts, and other similar ideas. These were tools that users installed on their browsers that would provide various library-related functionality to assist them on the web pages they were on.

For instance, the LibX toolbar, when integrated with your library catalog service, would convert DOIs and ISBNs on web pages into clickable links that, when clicked, would do a search of your system.[2] If set up correctly with the library's Summon discovery service, the user would receive an overlay with the results from the Summon discovery service displayed right on the web page when they hovered their mouse over such links! However, custom toolbars quickly became associated with malware, adware, and spyware, and they soon fell out of favor everywhere. In this section, we will discuss two more of these predecessor tools—the proxy bookmarklet and Unpaywall, which first introduced some of the functionality found in the current generation of access broker tools.

Proxy Bookmarklet

The original inventor of the concept of the proxy bookmarklet tool is unknown, but by 2010, variants of this tool with varying names could be found mentioned on many academic library sites. Figure 3.2 provides an example of the instructions given to set up the proxy bookmarklet for the author's institution.

But what did the proxy bookmarklet do and how did it work? Simply put, when you clicked on the bookmarklet, it would use JavaScript to append the EZproxy string to the URL of the page you were on. As we saw in chapter 2, doing this would allow you to reroute your access via the proxy server, giving you access to the item (if your institution had access, of course; see this workflow in figure 3.3).

As I noted in a presentation in 2013, when heavily promoted, the proxy bookmarklet technique can be very popular.[3] However, there are quite a few drawbacks that make promoting it difficult. First, the concept of bookmarklets is not a mainstream idea, and installing them is not intuitive. Though most libraries create guides on how to use bookmarklets, in my experience, many students struggled to install it without individual guidance from a library worker.

Second, the proxy bookmarklet does not work automatically; users have to remember to click on it to activate it. As users are not given any indication when they can use the proxy bookmarklet to access resources, they will not know in advance if clicking on the bookmarklet will allow them access; a novice user might try using it on every web page, and this can lead to a lot of frustration if they click on it and find they have no access most of the time.

Third, as we have seen, the proxy bookmarklet works by appending the proxy to a URL, which gives users access to resources via EZproxy. As we saw in chapter 2, this will allow the platform to recognize that the user is from the appropriate institution with the corresponding access rights. For example, clicking on the proxy bookmarklet on the JSTOR home page would only authenticate the user to JSTOR via their institution. It is critical to note that the institution may not have licensed access to every piece of content on the JSTOR platform, so even after this process, the user might still be frustrated that they can't access this specific JSTOR article. This often leads to confusion and frustration for the user, as they have already signed on to the JSTOR platform and yet still do not have access to the content. As you will see later, an article-level approach might work better.

Last, the proxy bookmarklet alone does not handle the appropriate copy problem. This can cause users of the bookmarklet to think that they do not have access to the content when they may be able to access it via alternative platforms. This is particularly problematic

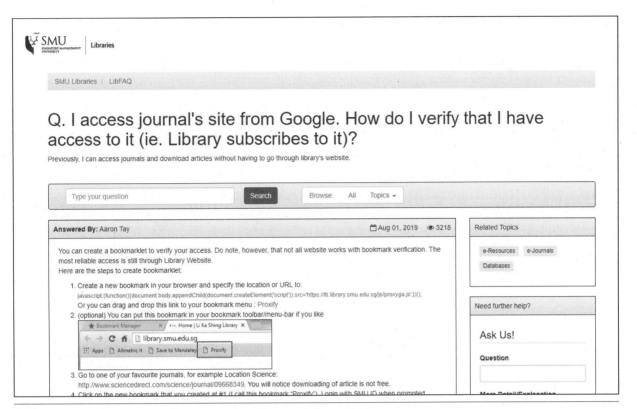

Figure 3.2
Instructions for setting up the proxy bookmarklet at the author's institution

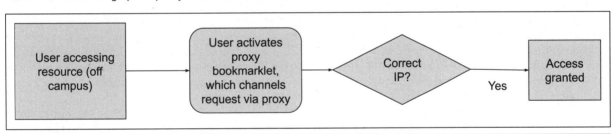

Figure 3.3
Granted access via proxy bookmarklet when accessing library resources off campus

for institutions that heavily provide access via aggregators like EBSCO or Ovid because such content might be missed. As you will see, the current generation of access broker browser extensions remedy some, if not most, of these problems.

Unpaywall Browser Extension

Clearly, one obvious improvement would be to convert the proxy bookmarklet to a browser extension, which would make it easier to install, use, and update and to track usage. This is where browser extensions like Unpaywall come in.

First appearing in 2017, browser extensions such as Unpaywall, Open Access Button, and CORE Discovery are designed to direct users to open-access versions of articles. They work by examining the metadata of the web pages users are on for article identifiers (e.g., DOI and PMID). This metadata, or article identifiers, is then used to find open-access copies, and if one is available, the user is directed to the full-text resource.

Open Access Button
https://openaccessbutton.org

CORE Discovery
https://core.ac.uk/services/discovery

In other words, Unpaywall and other similar tools worked on an item- or article-level approach to identify the article needed and check if a full-text copy was available, *no matter where it was*. As already alluded to, this solves part of the appropriate copy problem.

Table 3.1. Current access broker browser extensions

	Google Scholar Button	Lazy Scholar	Lean Library	LibKey Nomad	EndNote Click
Vendor	Google	Colby Vorland	Lean Library, a Sage publishing company	Third Iron	Clarivate
Business model	Free	Free	Subscription	Subscription	Freemium
Year launched	2015	2013	2016	2019	2017
Installations of Chrome extension as of Dec. 31, 2021	3 million+	10,000+	100,000+	200,000+	1 million+
Authentication supported	Same as Google Scholar Library Links program	EZproxy	EZproxy, OpenAthens, Shibboleth	EZproxy, OpenAthens, Shibboleth	EZproxy, OpenAthens, Shibboleth
Setup required by library	None if you are already set up in Google Scholar	None	Some	Some, minimal if you have BrowZine set up	Minimal
1 click to PDF	No	No	No	Yes	Yes
Supports DDS/ILL	No	No	Yes	Yes	Yes (with institutional bundle)
Some unique points	Free PDFs via Google Scholar	Recommendations, citation metrics	Supports e-book access Workflow integration with Springshare LibGuides, EDS, Summon, Primo, and Scite Widest support across different browsers	Integration with Retraction Watch Database LibKey integration with Wikipedia and selected databases such as PubMed, Scopus, Web of Science	PDF cloud storage COUNTER-compliant dashboard analytics (for institutions)

Also, unlike the proxy bookmarklet, Unpaywall and similar extensions work automatically and are activated whenever a free copy is found, without any input from the user, avoiding all the issues mentioned in the discussion of the proxy bookmarklet. Of course, as popular as browser extensions like these are, they could only bring the user to open-access copies and do not completely solve the appropriate copy problem.

The access broker browser extensions described in the next section attempt to solve the issue by using the same idea, but instead of just trying to find open-access copies, they also try to find institutionally accessible copies. In fact, the modern access broker browser extension typically works like this for access to journal articles:

1. It automatically looks for article identifiers or other metadata of the item on the page the user is on.
2. If an identifier is found, it checks if the user has access to the item via institutional access and, if so, pops up a badge with a link to the full-text copies.
3. If an identifier isn't available, the user is directed to open-access copies if any are available.
4. If all these methods fail, the user is typically given

additional options via the library link resolver, which usually include interlibrary loan or document delivery service (ILL/DDS).

Depending on the access broker in question and the setup, the authentication and authorization process for each user may occur differently, which is something we will discuss further in each product's section. Note that such an article-level approach works only for access to full-text journal articles but may not help with access to online resources such as abstracting and indexing databases or newspaper databases. Some access brokers, such as Lean Library, do provide alternative ways to support access.

Current Access Broker Browser Extensions

Today it is common for academic libraries to subscribe to one or more commercial access broker extensions while providing support for other free versions. The market for such products is developing very quickly. Table 3.1 provides a brief look at current options available. For a more robust list, please refer to my comparison page of access broker browser extensions, which is actively updated.

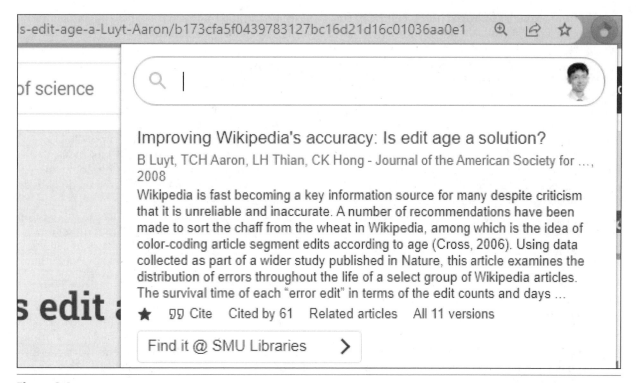

Figure 3.4
An example of Google Scholar Button pop-up when the user clicks on the extension

Comparison of Access Broker Browser Extensions
https://musingsaboutlibrarianship.blogspot.com/2019/07/a-comparison-of-6-access-broker-browser.html

Google Scholar Button

- **Pros:** Free. Minimal setup if already in Google Library Links program. Google Scholar is known to be one of the most capable tools for finding open-access articles, and this carries over to the Google Scholar Button extension.
- **Cons:** User has to click to activate. There is no support for ILL/DDS when an article is not available.

Looking for an easy-to-use and free browser extension? Google Scholar Button fits the bill! First launched by Google in 2015, this easy-to-use tool is by far the most popular access broker browser extension on the list with over three million installations! There is a possibility your researcher might even already be using it.

How does it work and how do you set it up? The only requirement for the Google Scholar Button to work with your institution's holdings is that your library is set up for Google's Library Links program.[4] It is highly likely that your library has already done so. Often, libraries set up a monthly update to upload library holdings to Google Scholar to participate in the program. Assuming the library is set up for Library Links, researchers can turn on this feature for their institution by setting up Google Scholar in the Library Links settings. This process will result in links to full text available via their institution appearing next to results in Google Scholar.

This feature works well, and it is often taken for granted by the millions of researchers who use Google Scholar. But one issue is that this feature works only on Google Scholar, so it will not help researchers who land on any other page. This is where the Google Scholar browser extension comes in. By installing it, you can bring this feature along with you. When you land on any article landing page for an article you cannot access, all you need to do is to click on the Google Scholar Button icon and the browser extension will attempt to

- check if there is an article title on the page you are in,
- send the title over to search Google Scholar, and
- if one or more articles match in Google Scholar, it will pop up and display the usual article-level linking made available by the Library Links programs.

On top of the links provided by the Google Scholar Library Links program, the user will also be shown the free PDFs found by Google Scholar. This helps supplement the copies available via institutional access (see figure 3.4 on p. 25 for an example). While other browser extensions have the same feature by utilizing external services such as Unpaywall, CORE OA Discovery, and so on, Google Scholar Button is often capable of finding additional free-to-read copies, using Google Scholar's own excellent open-access-finding capability.

Compared to the other access broker browser extensions, Google Scholar Button is missing two major features. First, this is the only access broker browser extension that requires the user to remember to click to activate the full-text-finding feature, while others do it automatically on every relevant page. Second, almost all the other browser extensions provide an option to a user (typically a route to ILL/DDS) if no institutional access is available, but this is not possible when using the Google Scholar Button.

Lazy Scholar

- **Pros:** Free. Many features, such as checking for comments on PubPeer, PDF extraction of information such as population, intervention, outcomes, funding, references. Pulls citation data at article and journal levels.
- **Cons:** Overcomplicated extension and user interface. Supported by private individual.

Lazy Scholar is unique in that it is created and supported by a private individual—Colby Vorland, currently a postdoc at Indiana University. It is provided at no charge. One of the earliest browser extensions in this class of products, the earliest version of Lazy Scholar worked in a similar manner to the Google Scholar Button and scraped links from the Google Scholar Library Links program to provide access. The current version provides an added access option, similar to the way EndNote Click works.

Today, Lazy Scholar has a multitude of features, including

- recommended papers
- extraction of metrics (altmetrics, CiteScore)
- checking PubPeer comments,
- two institutional full-text options, including "automatic institutional full-text access"
- autosaving and auto-renaming PDFs
- PDF extraction features, including extraction of references, outline of sections, conflict of interest and funders, and more

While Lazy Scholar is free to use, the fact that it is maintained by one individual and is not open source might lead to concerns about sustainability. Even if this was not an issue, Lazy Scholar is clearly a work of

passion, and the interface probably suffers due to the variety of features included.

Lean Library

- **Pros:** Works with e-books. Integration with various common library platforms, including library discovery services (Summon, Primo, EBSCO Discovery Service), Springshare LibGuides, and more. LibAssist function allows librarians to leave customizable messages based on domain or URL user visits.
- **Cons:** Additional functionality means more setup costs. No direct PDF linking. The additional features that help with added discovery of content might be overkill for users who know what they want and seek only delivery options.

Traditionally, many library products began as an idea in the library itself, and Lean Library was no different. Johan Tilstra, a library technologist working in Utrecht University Library, came up with the idea of a browser extension, then dubbed UU Easy Access browser extension, which was eventually spun off as an incubator start-up, Lean Library.[5] In 2018, Sage acquired Lean Library.

We met Utrecht University earlier in chapter 1 and mentioned its pitch about "thinking the unthinkable" and prioritizing delivery instead of discovery. Lean Library was one of the dividends of this thinking.[6] The early version consisted of three different modules, with the Easy Access module being the heart of the extension. This can be seen as an improvement over the classic proxy bookmarklet by addressing the main drawback of that tool. The problem with the classic proxy bookmarklet is that it requires the user to remember to click to apply the proxy on the web page the user is on. Another related issue is that even when the user remembers to do so, they might be greeted with an error when they try to go on sites to which they have no access. As mentioned earlier, while clicking the bookmarklet will append the EZproxy string to the URL, and hence channel access via the proxy server, the proxy server will do so only for a list of authorized domains (e.g., jstor.org, ScienceDirect.com). If this is tried on a site that isn't on the authorized list, the user will see an error that is often an uninformative pop-up. This can be confusing and a big turnoff.

Lean Library's improvement is that the extension will automatically offer to proxy the site the user is on when appropriate. How does the extension know when it is appropriate? The library defines a list of domains that is stored in the extension.

Lean Library has expanded to include other useful functions bundled in different modules. Some are by now standard in most access broker browser extensions, including article-level linking to open-access papers, using services such as CORE Discovery, and support of link resolvers and ILL/DDS. However, some are unique to Lean Library.

For example, the LibAssist module allows librarians to leave custom messages that pop up when users visit certain domains or even URLs. One could set up a message to inform users, while they may not have access to market reports on a particular website, users can search databases such as Passport or Statista for similar content. Or the library could pop up a message when users are on a specific database such as Scopus asking them for their feedback via a survey link to solicit feedback for renewal.

Another unique feature of Lean Library is that it is the only access broker product on the market that provides linking to e-books, though this feature isn't as mature as for journal articles. In 2022, Lean Library is promoting a new product called Lean Library Futures and Lean Library's Workflow for LibGuides, which can integrate with Springshare LibGuides and FAQs as well as three major library discovery services—Summon, EBSCO Discovery Service, and Primo.

Interestingly, a lot of these features focus on providing alternative discovery options as opposed to delivery options of what the user is currently looking for. For example, on a Google Scholar search page where you are searching for the phrase *social network*, you can mouse over a button generated by the extension and see an overlay of results for that same search from your library discovery service. This provides an alternative to what your Google Scholar search has offered.

This type of content integration works even for videos, so you could be on a YouTube page searching for *social networks* when Lean Library offers to show results from selected library video platforms such as Sage Video and JoVE. Even text on sites such as Wikipedia can be overlaid with definitions and taxonomies from sources such as Sage Research Methods or even Statista (a business database). Hovering your mouse over phrases or words will draw definitions or content from these sources. Finally, the new Lean Library Futures allows users to give feedback on licensed resources via Net Promoter Score and permits integration of badges and information from providers such as Altmetric and Scite. Lean Library provides a very comprehensive set of features, and overall it is quite a complete product.

In a way, these new features are the return to the Library 2.0 ideas of the early to mid-2000s, boasting all the bells and whistles that libraries can use to maintain a presence on users' browsers as they browse the web. This fact has two consequences. First, unlike the other access broker browser extensions, Lean Library has a lot more features to configure for the library setting it up. Second, from the user's point of view, if you are a senior researcher looking for a tool to quickly gain access to full-text papers (and offer DDS/ILL if a paper is not available), you might find all the additional popups and features distracting. As a result, this tool might be more suitable for students and less experienced searchers who need additional support beyond just streamlining delivery.

LibKey Nomad

- **Pros:** Provides holistic deep linking technologies beyond browser extensions. Is the only extension besides EndNote Click to offer "one-click to PDF" technology whenever possible. Has good support of aggregators (EBSCO and ProQuest).
- **Cons:** No additional discovery feature. Supports access to only journal articles, not databases or other online resources.

While Lean Library provides a host of useful supplementary services, you might be more interested in a service that has a razor focus just on improving delivery. This is where Third Iron's LibKey Nomad comes in. LibKey Nomad is the newest of the browser extensions profiled in this chapter. For many academic librarians, Third Iron is well known, being the company behind the highly popular BrowZine product, which allows academic and medical libraries to offer a consistent web and mobile interface to users who want to browse subscription and open-access journals. To develop BrowZine, Third Iron developed its own proprietary linking technology now dubbed LibKey to link users directly to full text.

Third Iron's website states that it offers "expert system full-text linking . . . [that] intelligently deliver[s] one-click access to millions of PDFs and HTML articles." Subscribers to the Third Iron suite of services will be able to use LibKey services to "eliminate the confusing maze of clicks to deliver the experience users expect, save researchers valuable time, and reduce help desk and ILL requests."[7] Of course, librarians reading this text might wonder how LibKey differs from existing library link-resolver technology (including OpenURL).

What is important to note is that the LibKey infrastructure does not claim to be a complete link-resolver solution. It specializes in handling full-text requests with article identifiers (specifically DOIs and PMIDs) and acts as "a Link Resolver Accelerator."[8] The idea here is that instead of covering the full range of full-text requests (some of which will not have article identifiers), LibKey will sit in front of your normal link-resolver solution and resolve such requests with article identifiers only. If LibKey is unable to resolve the request for full text, the request will be passed on to the normal link-resolver solution. While linking via identifiers seems to be a relatively easy process for link resolvers, things get harder if the institution's access is via aggregators, and this is where Third Iron claims that its "dynamic link construction dramatically improves reliability of linking to other aggregated sources, minimizing common linking errors such as in press articles."[9] For example, unlike most of the other services on this list, it has its own proprietary linking to aggregators such as ProQuest and EBSCOhost (one-click PDF linking). As an added benefit, full-text articles requested via LibKey are checked for retractions via the Retraction Watch Database, and users will be warned if there is a hit.

The LibKey suite of services consists of

- LibKey Link
- LibKey Discovery
- LibKey.io
- LibKey Nomad

All four services utilize the LibKey linking technology in different contexts. LibKey Link functions as a link-resolver accelerator, which you can use in place of your usual link resolver in databases such as Scopus, Web of Science, and even PubMed (via Library LinkOut using Outside Tool[10]). As mentioned earlier, the service will try to resolve full-text DOI and PMID requests via LibKey first before passing on to the normal link resolver if necessary. LibKey Discovery is meant to be used in most major library discovery services, including EBSCO Discovery Service, Primo, Summon, and WorldCat.

LibKey.io is reminiscent of Sci-Hub in terms of functionality even though it is legal. Go to the website, enter a DOI or PMID, select an institution, and you will be brought to the full text if it is available. Doing so will set a cookie in your browser, so you will not have to select your institution again. Similar to LibKey Link, if LibKey.io fails to find full-text options, it will generate a library access option that usually goes to the library link resolver. Ultimately, to use LibKey.io for your institution, simply point your browser to this URL:

https://libkey.io/libraries/{LibraryID}/{DOI or PMID}

So, for example, for my institution you need to go to

https://libkey.io/libraries/646/10.1017/S104909
6511000199.

This URL works as well:

https://libkey.io/{DOI or PMID}

However, in this instance, the user will be asked to select an institution, if they have not done so before.

LibKey Linking is also natively supported by various databases and services. A short list includes Semantic Scholar, Scholarcy, CAB Direct, and the literature-mapping tool Inciteful.

Last, we come to LibKey Nomad, the access broker browser extension. It is very similar to the other extensions we have already considered. Once installed, it sits quietly in the user's browser and will activate when the user lands on an appropriate page, showing a badge with a link to the full text if LibKey Nomad detects that full text is available. Like all the other services, it will also direct you to open-access copies if they are available.

If full text is not available either way, then it will show another option called Access Options, which typically links to the institution's link resolver. Installing the LibKey Nomad extension also brings additional functionality. For example, when a user is browsing Wikipedia, the references in the reference sections of the page will be overlaid with full-text links when possible, and this feature extends to other popular abstracting and indexing (A&I) databases such as Scopus, Web of Science, PubMed, and so on.

Third Iron's suite of products is very focused and enhances the reliability of your link resolvers. Setup is relatively easy, particularly if you have already set up the BrowZine product; otherwise, it provides support for most popular electronic resource management systems, such as Alma and Serial Solutions, to sync your holdings. It is important to note that the LibKey suite of products assists users with access to article content only. While this covers a lot of what users might be looking for, it will not help users who need help accessing non-journal content such as e-books. Nor will it help the user to sign on to non-full-text platforms and databases such as Scopus or Artstor, unlike Lean Library.

EndNote Click (formerly Kopernio)

- **Pros:** Almost no setup required. Good one-click PDF linking.
- **Cons:** May not cover aggregators (e.g., EBSCO) well. Requires saving of username and password in extension. Extension also uses username and password on behalf of user, which may infringe some institutions' IT use policy.

Kopernio, which is now known as EndNote Click, was also an early entrant. It began as a start-up by Jan Reichelt and Ben Kaube in 2017 before eventually being acquired by Clarivate in April 2018.

When it launched, the product garnered a lot of press and publicity and became very popular in researcher circles. It was, and still is, offered as a freemium product from the very start, which explains how it racked up one million installations compared to

Lean Library's 100,000+ and Third Iron's 200,000+ installations of LibKey Nomad, which required an institutional subscription to fully benefit from their features.

EndNote Click's basic functionality should be very familiar by now. It's a browser extension that sits in the browser and will pop up a badge with the text "View PDF" (see figure 3.5 for an example). Clicking on it will link you to full text if it can find a copy available via your institution. Like the other browser extensions, it can also link you to open-access copies of papers.

For many institutions that have set it up, it will also offer additional options if no full-text option is available (including open-access copies). Typically, it will send users to the link-resolver options if it is unable to find full text.

EndNote Click was the first access broker browser extension to tout the advantage of "one click to PDF" functionality, and today it may still be the best at this functionality. As with LibKey Nomad, installing the extension will result in the extension overlaying popular websites such as Wikipedia and databases such as PubMed with buttons that are links to PDF files.

In terms of unique functionality, EndNote Click provides a "locker" that allows users to store in the cloud PDFs that they have downloaded via the extension. EndNote Click is the only access broker browser extension offered as a freemium product. Choosing to pay as an individual will increase cloud storage as well as providing additional functionality such as syncing to Dropbox; however, if you do not use this feature, EndNote Click is perfectly functional as a free service. EndNote Click leverages its position as a Clarivate company with integration with other Clarivate products, including EndNote and Web of Science, but otherwise it works similarly to other access broker extensions.

While this product feels very similar to other access brokers already introduced—particularly Lib-Key Nomad—from the back end EndNote Click works quite differently. For access broker browser extensions to work, the access broker usually needs to work with each institution. Whether it be the need to get a holdings file of what the institution has coverage of or the institution's OpenURL path, some setup needs to be done. In the case of LibKey Nomad and Lean Library, there is a need to send a list of your institution's holdings to the access broker vendors before the extension works. Even in the case of the Google Scholar Button or Lazy Scholar, where the feature appears to work automatically, these extensions work by leveraging the work institutions are already doing by working with Google Scholar in the Library Links program.

Yet many institutions may be surprised to find that despite their not working with EndNote Click directly, the extension may be already fully functional for their users even if their institutions do not provide coverage

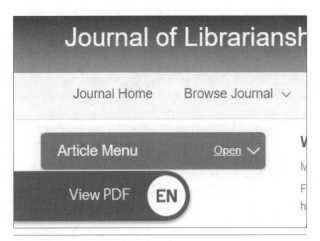

Figure 3.5
An example of EndNote Click's pop-up badge

data. Indeed, unlike other services in this list, no setup is needed to indicate your holdings, which is a great time saver. How this works is described on the End-Note Click web page, but essentially, it will use your users' stored credentials in real time to check if they have access to the full text. The trade-off for this is that your users will need their user accounts and passwords saved in the application, which EndNote Click will use to check journal websites directly for full-text access. While Clarivate assures us that all user credentials are encrypted, stored in your local browser cache, and never "sent to EndNote Click and never leave your browser other than to be submitted to the verified institutional authentication service," some people might still have privacy concerns.[11]

One other disadvantage of EndNote Click is that it prioritizes full-text access from publishers' platforms and provides little aggregator support. As of the time of this writing (March 2022), it supports ProQuest as an aggregator but not EBSCOhost and may not be suitable for an institution that provides access to journal content largely via EBSCO only.

Ultimately, though EndNote Click can provide access to full text without additional work by the institution, the product works better with official institutional involvement. For example, the institution can add additional options if no full text is found and also has access to an institutional dashboard that shows the pattern of downloads from its users of the extension. This helps with figuring out which titles are popular, how many of the PDFs that are downloaded are publisher-hosted versus OA alternatives, and more.

Why Not Access Broker Browser Extensions?

While access broker browser extensions appear to be a great way to improve user access and delivery options,

Library Technology Reports   alatechsource.org   August/September 2022

they have some drawbacks. The first is a practical one. Your users will not by default have the browser extension installed, and while some institutions, such as the University of Manchester, have achieved some degree of success with high penetration rates with their user base, this usually can't be achieved without a fair degree of marketing effort.[12] Working with your institution's IT department to see if there is some mass auto-deployment method available (e.g., via Microsoft Group Policy) might be advisable.[13]

The other objection to the widespread deployment of access broker browser extensions is concern about privacy issues that browser extensions might bring. One of the strongest cases against this class of products was made by the group known as RA21. This group has since been followed by a successor organization, SeamlessAccess, whose work we will discuss in detail in chapter 4. In "RA21 Position Statement on Access Brokers," the group, which also coined the phrase *access brokers*, took aim at some of these tools and argued that

- these tools may have potential security risks as some of them store users' institutional usernames and passwords;
- they often require the creation of individual accounts, leading to privacy risks; and
- they generally enable providers of these tools to track "end user behavior and reading habits across publisher sites potentially impacting privacy and research freedom."[14]

Ultimately, RA21 claims that such tools, while useful in the short term, do not actually fundamentally solve the issue. As we will see in the next chapter, RA21 aims to solve this problem by working on and implementing a long-term fundamental solution by building on federated identity management practices.

Conclusion

In this chapter, we covered the history of access broker browser extensions and introduced five popular tools that institutions have been using to help users with access. Consisting of both free tools (Google Scholar and Lazy Scholar) and commercial tools (Lean Library, LibKey Nomad, and EndNote Click), they are must-have tools in the arsenal of academic libraries today. However, as noted in the last section, these tools are not a complete solution as they require our users to be aware of them and to install them, and they may create privacy and security risks. RA21,

now succeeded by SeamlessAccess, argues that such tools are at best a temporary Band-Aid and that we are better off with solutions that improve the way we authenticate and authorize users to access resources. We shall turn our attention to that next.

Notes

1. RA21: Resource Access for the 21st Century, "RA21 Position Statement on Access Brokers," August 23, 2018, https://ra21.org/what-is-ra21/ra21-position-state ment-on-access-brokers/.
2. Galadriel Chilton and Joelle Thomas, "LibX: The Small but Mighty Button for E-Resource Discovery and Access," *Serials Librarian* 66, no. 1–4 (2014): 146–52, https://doi.org/10.1080/0361526X.2014.879019.
3. Aaron Tay, "Starting Research from Outside the Library Homepage: An Analysis of User Behavior from an Academic Library" (presentation, IFLA 2013 Satellite Meeting on Literacy and Reference Services, National Library Board, Singapore, August 2013).
4. "Library Support," Google Scholar Help, accessed October 5, 2021, https://scholar.google.com/intl/en /scholar/libraries.html.
5. Johan Tilstra, "Lean Library's Browser Extension: Seamless Delivery for Users," *Aaron Tay's Musings about Librarianship* (blog), May 30, 2017, http://mus ingsaboutlibrarianship.blogspot.com/2017/05/guest -post-lean-librarys-browser.html.
6. Simone Kortekaas and Bianca Kramer, "Thinking the Unthinkable: Doing Away with the Library Catalogue," *Insights* 27, no. 3 (November 3, 2014): 244–48, https://doi.org/10.1629/2048-7754.174.
7. Third Iron home page, https://thirdiron.com.
8. Third Iron, "LibKey Link Technical FAQ," accessed June 13, 2022, https://support.thirdiron.com/knowledgebase /articles/1947991-libkey-link-technical-faq.
9. Third Iron home page.
10. For more information, see M. Collins, "PubMed Labs Update: Library LinkOut using Outside Tool," *NLM Technical Bulletin,* no. 429 (July–August 2019), https:// www.nlm.nih.gov/pubs/techbull/ja19/ja19_pubmed_ labs_linkout.html.
11. "EndNote Click: How Does EndNote Click Store and Protect Institutional Credentials?," Clarivate Support, April, 9, 2021, https://support.clarivate.com/Endnote /s/article/EndNote-Click-How-does-EndNote-Click -store-and-protect-institutional-credentials.
12. Third Iron, "How the University of Manchester Library Reduced Support Ticket Volume by 25%," case study, 2020, https://thirdiron.com/wp-content/uploads/2020 /02/University-of-Manchester-case-study.pdf.
13. Third Iron, "Libkey Nomad Group Policy Deployment (Edge)," accessed October 11, 2021, https://support .thirdiron.com/knowledgebase/articles/1970322-lib key-nomad-group-policy-deployment-edge.
14. RA21: Resource Access for the 21st Century, "RA21 Position Statement," para. 7.

Chapter 4

Improving Authentication and Authorization

SeamlessAccess and GetFTR

Introduction

In chapter 2, we talked briefly about SAML-based methods for authentication and authorization. However, IP recognition, despite all its drawbacks, is still the more common way of providing access. Why is this so?

Why RA21 or SeamlessAccess?

Here is a recap of how SAML works. Refer to the section Single Sign-on with SAML in chapter 2 for a fuller description.

Imagine a user is on JSTOR and tries to read a specific article. To activate the SAML-based method, also known as single sign-on (SSO), the user clicks on the sign-on button or link and identifies the institution they are from. This is typically done by selecting from a list of institutions. This sign-in process is known as the Where-Are-You-From (WAYF) process.

JSTOR, which acts as the service provider (SP), then redirects the user to the identity provider (IdP) of the institution, which we will call Institution X, for authentication.

How does JSTOR know where the IdP of Institution X is? Either Institution X has worked directly with JSTOR to provide the address of the IdP, or both the SP and Institution X are in the same identity federation (see chapter 2 for a discussion on what an identity federation is) and JSTOR looks up the address in the SAML directory.

Either way, the user authenticates using their institutional credentials at the IdP of Institution X. Assuming this goes well, the user is redirected back to the SP with a SAML assertion. The assertion may contribute *attributes* that contain information about the user. (We'll discuss this more later.) The SP then gives access to the user (see figure 4.1).

What types of SAML assertions and attributes can be sent by the IdP? In one scenario, the IdP can simply assert the user is affiliated with Institution X and entitled to the rights from such an affiliation.[1] In such a scenario, the anonymous identifier is unique for every visit and the SP. This is the highest level of privacy provided to the user in this process, as the SP does not get any information at all about the user beyond their institutional status.

Sometimes users from the same institution may have different entitlements depending on the department they are from. Additional assertations could assert that the user is from Institution X and also is an associate professor from Department Y. In this situation, the SAML assertation from the IdP to the SP would include some information about the user, possibly identifying the user's department or user group in an attribute. There's a possibility, of course, that liberal release of such attributes might allow users to be identifiable in practice. In the most extreme case, personally identifiable information (PII)—such as campus e-mail, name, and position—can be asserted and the information sent as attributes to the SP, which of course would allow individual users to be tracked. Finally, the IdP may make assertations that involve release of pseudonymous identifiers. They are similar to anonymous identifiers, except that while anonymous identifiers are generated for each visit, pseudonymous identifiers are generated for each person/SP combination; they persist and are reused across visits. In other words, if pseudonymous identifiers are used in the SAML process, the SP will always know it is the same user who is accessing the service but will not know the real identity of the user based on the identifier alone. This approach can be useful in cases where the user wants personalization (e.g., saving the custom settings of their account) but not to be personally identifiable.

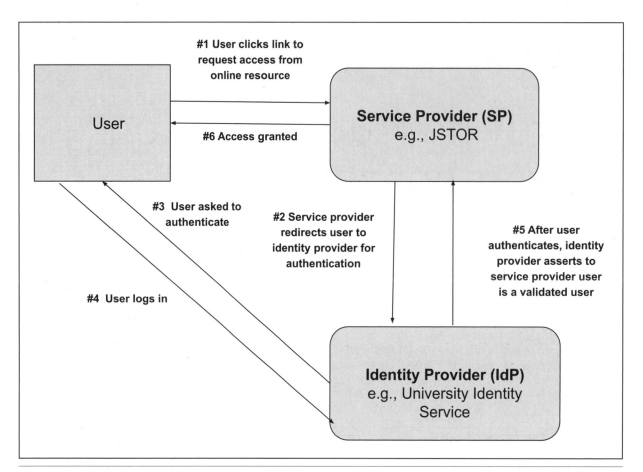

Figure 4.1
Diagram of the SAML SSO process

All this is fine as far as it goes. However, use of SAML-based methods is still not widespread.[2] Why? Besides the fact that not all library-licensed resources support SAML, there are a couple of reasons. First, while I have painted an ideal picture of how SAML-based federated access is supposed to work, in practice users find it unintuitive to use due to inconsistent and poor user interface (UI) elements during the IdP discovery phase. Second, the library may prefer IP authentication for a variety of reasons, including

- librarian lack of familiarity with federated access methods
- librarian concern about user privacy issues, perhaps driven by the lack of standardization in attribute release standards

RA21: Resource Access for the 21st Century was formed to explore solutions to some of these issues.

The IDP Discovery or the WAYF Problem

Launched in 2016, RA21 was a joint initiative of the International Association of Scientific, Technical, and Medical Publishers (STM) and NISO with this mission: "to align and simplify pathways to subscribed content across participating scientific platforms. RA21 will address the common problems users face when interacting with multiple and varied information protocols."[3]

Though this mission sounds somewhat vague, RA21 aimed to "explore pathways to move beyond IP-recognition as the primary authentication system." In practice, this means RA21 focused quickly on improving user experience for researchers using SAML methods. It completed its initiative on June 30, 2019, with the publication of the NISO *Recommended Practices for Improved Access to Institutionally-Provided Information Resources.*[4] Chief among the recommendations was setting up a new service, SeamlessAccess, to carry out the recommendations.

For the rest of the discussion, we will use just SeamlessAccess as a catchall term to describe the work of RA21 and the successor organization SeamlessAccess. SeamlessAccess identified several areas of improvement for SAML-based sign-ons but aims to improve and standardize sign-in UI across all platforms. It particularly focused on improving the WAYF,

Figure 4.2
SeamlessAccess standardized log-in button (sample)

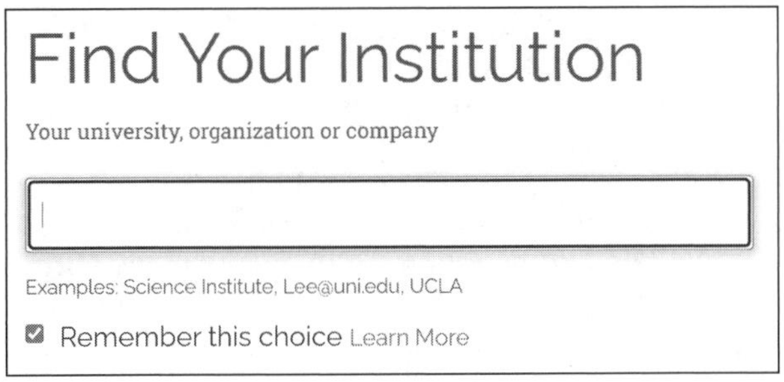

Find Your Institution

Your university, organization or company

Examples: Science Institute, Lee@uni.edu, UCLA

☑ Remember this choice Learn More

Figure 4.3
Search-based list box where users can identify their institution (sample)

or Where-Are-You-From, process as this was clearly a pain point. This is because prior to RA21 different journal publishers implemented this process in a nonstandard, unintuitive, and often confusing way. For example, users would often be faced with multiple WAYF options resulting in two or more ways to search for their institutions.

By carefully analyzing the difficulty users had with this process and coming up with guidelines for a simpler, more intuitive, and consistent UI across all platforms, SeamlessAccess hoped to make this problem far less significant. See figure 4.2 for an example of the standardized log-in button that will be implemented consistently across all platforms that support SeamlessAccess.

As noted by researchers, SAML-based implementations prior to implementing SeamlessAccess could be extremely unintuitive. For example, a Georgetown University nursing student compared the experience she had using SAML log-in on Wiley before and after Wiley switched to supporting SeamlessAccess as "night and day."[5] Some of the problems identified in the old sign-in included an excessive number of clicks needed, the need to scroll down a long list of institutions, and unnecessary use of jargon like "selecting a federation."

In comparison, the new SeamlessAccess UI, based on careful user testing, is a lot more intuitive with a consistent visual cue and call to action ("Access through your institution"). It normalizes the language used and provides a search-based list so users can easily find their institution (see figure 4.3).

There are also guidelines for responsive design to support mobile use. Because selecting the institution was often the slowest part of the process, SeamlessAccess also built in a browser-based mechanism that would allow the user's browser to remember the last

 Add or change institution

Figure 4.4
Institution preselected by browser

used sign-in and auto-populate that option by default. This information is similar to a cookie but is instead stored in browser local storage. The browser remembers which institution the user previously chose to sign in and selects that institution across sessions, and SPs that supported SeamlessAccess did the same, which saved the user a lot of time. (See figure 4.4 for what a user might see if information is stored in the browser about the last selected institution.)

With more and more platforms supporting SeamlessAccess, consistency will help users know what to expect—the same way users today know what to do when faced with a Log in with Google or Facebook button. Still, for SeamlessAccess to work, platforms need to implement it.

Currently SeamlessAccess provides three types of integration for platforms that implement it—Limited, Standard, and Advanced methods. Please refer to the description of the service on the SeamlessAccess website for more details.

> *SeamlessAccess: The Service*
> https://seamlessaccess.org/services/

Publishers, such as IOPscience, that implemented SeamlessAccess have found large improvements. For example, IOPscience found that in 2021, total item requests via federated authentication increased by 82 percent after it implemented SeamlessAccess.[6]

Attribute Release and Privacy Concerns about SeamlessAccess

One of the major concerns librarians have about moving from IP recognition to SAML and the SeamlessAccess service is privacy and the attributes sent to SPs. The important thing to note is that the SP can receive only the attributes that the IdP releases. The question then becomes, Who decides what attributes should be sent? While the SP and IdP can mutually agree on the attributes to be sent (including, as noted earlier, none at all, in which case an anonymous identifier assertion is sent), it seems that it would be easier if there were some standards to follow.

This is where entity categories come into play, and a federation can define and use these categories to set standards for SPs and IdPs in that federation. An example of such an entity category would be REFEDS's (Research and Education Federations) Research and Scholarship (R&S) entity category, which would apply a set of standard attribute release criteria for all SPs classed under this category, but this does not apply to library-licensed resources.

This has led to the development, under the auspices of SeamlessAccess, of the new Anonymous Authorization and Pseudonymous Authorization entity categories.[7] Despite this development, many are still skeptical about supporting SAML-based methods and whether they should replace IP recognition and proxy servers.

In chapter 2, we saw IP recognition and proxy servers were extremely inconvenient for users, particularly off campus; however, they have one major advantage in that user's privacy is protected. Access via the proxy ensured that SPs would get practically no information on who was accessing the content as everything was filtered via the proxy.

While it is true that SAML access can be configured such that the usage is mostly anonymous and the SP is told only that the user is a legitimate user of the institution (through release of an anonymous identifier generated per visit), it is possible for the user to be tracked with other exchanges of attributes as discussed earlier.

All in all, protecting user privacy is an extremely technically complicated and tricky topic with much potential for missteps, and concerned librarians worry about making a mistake. Below are just some scenarios that may lead to privacy issues:

- The IdP server is often not controlled directly by the library itself but by the institution, typically the campus IT department.[8] This might lead to misconfigurations that result in identifying information being leaked. Such misconfigurations are hard for the library to fix.[9]
- The people running the campus-wide IdP service may not share the same ethical and moral standard as libraries and may not see protecting user privacy as a concern.
- Even persistent pseudonymous identifiers might allow users to be tracked, as some have argued vendors can use a combination of web bugs and behavioral tracking to tie the persistent pseudonymous identifier to a real identity.[10]

Current Status of SeamlessAccess

At the time of writing in March 2022, SeamlessAccess is supported by about twenty service providers, including Elsevier's ScienceDirect, Wiley, Taylor & Francis, and the American Chemical Society (ACS), among others.[11] However, work needs to be done, not just from the publisher side, but also from the institutional side. For institutions to benefit from SeamlessAccess, their users need to be encouraged to try to access content from content owners that support it. On the back end, the library or institution itself also needs to be registered in the appropriate identity federation with its IdP, and the publisher needs to be in the same federation. It is not unusual for libraries to have no say in the management of the IdP, as this is usually under the control of the institution's campus IT department, so setting this up may not be simple from the library point of view.

Leaving aside technical capabilities, there is still concern about privacy. While the development of the Anonymous Authorization and Pseudonymous Authorization entity categories creates some clarification on the attribute release bundles, some librarians are still skeptical of federated access compared to IP authentication for the privacy reasons discussed earlier.

It is important to note that RA21 and, presumably, its successor SeamlessAccess have stated that they do indeed have a long-term goal of eliminating accessing resources via IP.[12] So, in the long term, this may not be a case of having an additional option that you can choose to ignore. To be fair, supporters of RA21/SeamlessAccess point out that IP-based methods that generally also require the use of proxies have other drawbacks even if we are willing to accept the friction they involve when the user isn't on campus. Use of proxies on today's internet increases complexity and may even permit certain security risks.

We now turn our attention to GetFTR, a publisher-initiated project targeted at improving delivery from another angle.

What Is GetFTR?

On December 3, 2019, five major publishers—ACS, Elsevier, Springer Nature, Taylor & Francis, and Wiley—announced the launch of the GetFTR project.[13] While RA21/SeamlessAccess focused on authentication, GetFTR focuses on streamlining access to journal content by means of real-time entitlement checks for users who discover such content via platforms other than the publisher website. This includes use of discovery tools (e.g., Scopus) and scholarly collaborative networks (e.g., Mendeley).

From the user's point of view, imagine being on a platform like Scopus and, after doing a search, seeing ten article results displayed and not knowing which article you have access to. The platform needs to reliably tell users which of these articles they have access to. Of course, part of this process involves the platform, known in GetFTR jargon as the *integrator service*, needing to confirm and authenticate the user. GetFTR does not do anything novel here. Instead, it uses the existing authentication mechanics—either IP

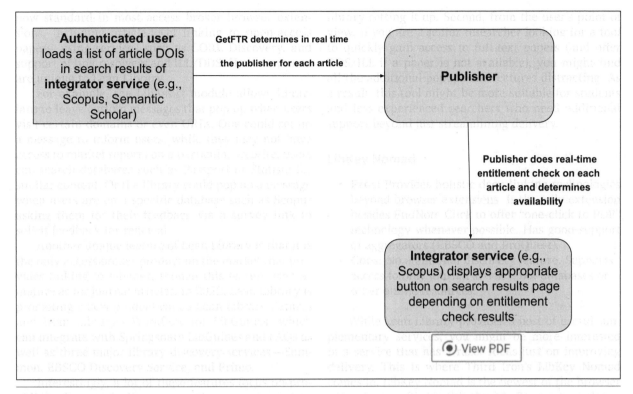

Figure 4.5
Workflow diagram for GetFTR

recognition or SAML-based methods, which include SeamlessAccess, as described earlier. What is novel is that once the platform authenticates the user, platforms that support GetFTR do real-time entitlement checks with GetFTR-supported publishers to get accurate and up-to-date information on whether the user can access the content and to display the information accordingly.

Note: Pre-authentication or lack of authentication will likely result in GetFTR displaying open-access or at least free-to-read full-text links.

GetFTR Explained Briefly

On paper, GetFTR works simply. See figure 4.5 for a workflow diagram.

GetFTR needs two pieces of information from the integrator service: the article DOI and the user's institution affiliation. The latter is obtained in a variety of ways, including

- SAML (or even SeamlessAccess) log-ins
- IP recognition

Next, for every article displayed with a DOI in the user's search, the GetFTR API will simply use the DOI to check which publisher it belongs to (via the Crossref API) and then route the query to the article publisher (publishers who are GetFTR partners) to see if the

user is entitled to it and display the availability next to each article. The process where it queries publishers to see if the user is entitled to a journal article is the real-time entitlement check. The publisher returns a corresponding *entitlement resource*, which contains the following pieces of information[14]:

- level of entitlement (e.g., yes, no)
- access type (e.g., open, free, paid)
- document type (e.g., version of record or alternative version)
- content type (e.g., HTML, PDF)
- a link to the actual resource

This information is then used by the integrator service to display the appropriate message on the search interface. Similar to SeamlessAccess, GetFTR has recommended callouts and labels to use consistently across all platforms. See figure 4.6 for the standardized GetFTR button that will be shown when the user is entitled to access the full text.

After a user has authenticated, the system is able to know by checking with the publisher whether the user is supposed to have access or not without the user even clicking through the link.[15] GetFTR seems to work similarly to traditional library link resolvers by facilitating user access to links that they can use to access full text regardless of where the resource is. In other words, both provide a solution to the so-called appropriate copy problem, so let's discuss that next. For a summary of how the following solutions to the appropriate copy problem stack up, see table 4.1.

Figure 4.6
Standard Get-FTR button displayed when a user is entitled to access full text

Figure 4.7
Google Scholar results where only one of two results has a link displayed

GetFTR and Solutions to the Appropriate Copy Problem

As we discussed in chapter 2, one of the more interesting issues about digital copies is that there might be more than one online site where a user can get access to a journal article. While a journal article may be available at the publisher site—say, Wiley—it may also be available to some users at aggregator sites such as EBSCOhost. These days there might also be open-access copies (of varying versions) available at preprint servers and institutional or subject repository sites. A user from Institution A might have access via one site, while a user from Institution B might have access via another site due to different licensing agreements. How does the system know where to send the user? This in a nutshell is what librarians called the appropriate copy problem in the early 2000s.

The creation of the library link resolvers and the OpenURL standard was intended to solve this issue. Platforms that supported this standard and armed with the right institutional context would direct users to the appropriate institutional link resolver, and users would eventually be fed the right link to the appropriate copy.

Traditional Solution to the Appropriate Copy Problem: Link Resolvers and OpenURL

In chapter 2, we discussed how the traditional solution to the appropriate copy problem was via library link resolvers, which typically use OpenURL technology. However, both traditional link-resolvers using OpenURL and GetFTR require some way to check to see what the user (who is already authenticated) is entitled to access and from which sites. In fact, this is the key difference between the two. In the case of traditional link resolvers, the information on entitlements is drawn from the library—more specifically from the library's knowledge base. In comparison, GetFTR queries the publisher directly.

Another, smaller difference is the way the links are implemented. In most cases, link resolver links today are displayed as static buttons on web pages that support the link resolver. The user will see the same button or link for each article and will need to click on the link before they know if they have access. GetFTR links are designed to be dynamic. When the page loads, the system will do a check on the fly and display different links or buttons depending on the

outcome of the entitlement check. This allows users to see what they have access to without first clicking on the link, which helps reduce frustration.

The closest traditional link resolvers come to supporting this feature is via the implementation of the Google Scholar Library Links program. When a user clicks on a displayed link in Google Scholar, they experience the same thing as they do on other platforms supporting library link resolvers. However, instead of displaying the same link next to every result, Google Scholar displays a link only for results where the user has access. See figure 4.7 for an example where one result has a link displayed (Find it @ SMU Libraries) and the other does not because Google Scholar knows the user is not entitled to access to the second resource via their institution. It can do so because Google Scholar obtains a local copy (which is updated periodically) of the institution's holdings or entitlements in advance and uses that to determine when to show a link.

Why GetFTR's Solution to the Appropriate Copy Problem Might Be Better

Why do we need GetFTR? How well do traditional library link resolvers work? After close to two decades' use of library link resolvers (which are largely but not entirely based on OpenURL technology), the main finding is that while OpenURL linking mostly works, it is not always reliable.[16] There are various reasons for this, but here I will highlight two relevant ones.

The first problem is specific to the way knowledge bases and the link resolvers that use them are set up. Knowledge bases record entitlement at the journal or source level and not at the article level. In other words, the knowledge bases, if written in plain English, would say something like "We are entitled to access articles from Journal X, from volume 1 to volume 20, via JSTOR and from volume 25 onward via Business Source Complete." They are unable to reflect variance of access within the same issue or volume.

You might wonder why this could be an issue. After all, libraries generally subscribe to journal articles by year (or volume and issue) and not by article. However, with the rise of open access and in

Table 4.1. Different solutions to the appropriate copy problem

Solution	Source of entitlements/holdings check	Final link to full text	Type of links displayed on website
Library link resolver	Library knowledge base	Provided by library link resolver	Typically displays the same static button or link. Checks for availability only on user click.
Google Scholar Library Links program (library link resolver)	Google Scholar's local copy of institution holdings	Provided by library link resolver	Google Scholar uses local copy of institution holdings to selectively display links.
GetFTR	Publisher	Provided by GetFTR publisher	Dynamic link. Checks for availability on load of page and displays appropriate links.
LibKey.io	LibKey.io, with holdings obtained periodically from library	LibKey link resolver	Typically displays the same static button or link. Checks for availability only on user click.

particular hybrid open access, we are starting to see authors pay for some articles to be made open access so that only those articles are free to read while others in the same issue are not. Clearly, because library link resolvers work mostly with the entitlement data in the knowledge base (at the journal or source level), they are unable to handle the case where some articles are open access and hence available to use while others in the same issue are behind paywalls.

Beyond this problem, the biggest stumbling block when using link resolvers is that it is simply very labor-intensive for libraries to keep their entitlements in the knowledge base up-to-date. When a library signs a contract with a publisher that gives the institution access to a journal package, librarians need to update the library's knowledge base with information about these new journals. This allows the link resolver to correctly recognize that users have access to these journals.

Unfortunately, ensuring that the library's knowledge base is accurate can be difficult since it involves the librarian keep tracking of hundreds of packages consisting of thousands of journals with different coverage entitlements across dozens of publishers that all change across time. This is not made easier by the fact that libraries may have their own unique package of titles, all of which requires the librarian to ensure that this information is correctly reflected in their library's knowledge base. While there have been advancements that speed up the process of updating the library's knowledge base (in particular with NISO's *KBART Automation: Automated Retrieval of Customer Electronic Holdings*, which libraries can use to automate population of supported knowledge bases instantly using the publisher's API), this still relies on the librarian updating the system.[17]

So what does GetFTR bring to the table? Instead of querying the library knowledge base, GetFTR cuts out the intermediary by simply querying the publishers for entitlements directly. Therefore, even if the library is delayed in updating its knowledge base, the moment the ink on the contract is dry, the access rights are updated on the publisher side and the user gets full access to the new entitlements without requiring the library to do any work.

As mentioned earlier, GetFTR also has another advantage over traditional link resolvers in that access is checked on the article level. This enables GetFTR to flag a hybrid article as available even if not all the articles in the same issue are accessible. That said, modern link resolvers don't use just OpenURL technology for linking but may also use other methods, such as integration of open-access-finding services like Unpaywall or CORE Discovery, that can help mitigate this issue. In addition, journal publishers do occasionally turn on free access for limited periods for various reasons such as promotion. Even if this free promotion were given only at the issue and volume level and hence could be captured in the knowledge base, it is unlikely that any library would make the effort to update its knowledge base for temporary access. This would not be a problem if a library uses GetFTR, as entitlements are managed automatically at the publisher level.

GetFTR's Solution vs. LibKey

In chapter 3, we discussed Third Iron's LibKey infrastructure and suite of services, and of all the solutions discussed, it is most like GetFTR. Like GetFTR, it works on the article level (unlike traditional link resolvers using OpenURL) and, more specifically, works on DOIs. Hence it can detect hybrid articles directly while link resolvers cannot.

Unlike GetFTR, LibKey supports some aggregators, such as ProQuest and EBSCOhost. Also unlike GetFTR, it integrates with link resolvers by passing on requests when it fails to find any hits. On the other hand, like other library solutions, it relies on the library's record of entitlements (which it gets a local copy of periodically), which can be incomplete for reasons already stated.

One thing to note is that while we have generally acted as if getting entitlements from the publisher is superior compared to getting entitlements from the library knowledge base, publisher-provided entitlements can be wrong too! As a result, it is important not to blindly trust that the publishers have made no errors in turning on entitlements and to ensure that procedures are in place to check on the accuracy of GetFTR linking.

Concerns about GetFTR

It is fair to say librarians expressed quite a bit of concern about GetFTR when it was first announced.[18] GetFTR moved quickly to address some of these concerns. For example, on first launch, it seemed tied to RA21/SeamlessAccess for authentication, which as noted earlier has its own set of issues, and this was addressed by announcing it would also allow support of IP authentication as well. On the community governance front, GetFTR was initially started by and involved only publishers. The lack of representatives from various other stakeholders, such as the researcher and librarian communities, was concerning. This issue has since been addressed as well, with noted librarian Lisa Hinchliffe among others nominated to serve on GetFTR's advisory board. However, other concerns remain.

First, questions were raised on whether GetFTR would also cover third-party aggregators and not just publishers. This is important to many institutions that have coverage of important journals via aggregators such as EBSCO or ProQuest rather than via publishers. While GetFTR issued an announcement almost immediately after its launch stating that "GetFTR is fully committed to supporting third-party aggregators,"[19] at the time of this writing in March 2022, this issue still has not been resolved and no aggregator is yet included. Related to this issue is the concern that GetFTR planned to show No Access labels (and might provide publisher-mandated options) if the GetFTR entitlement checks showed no access. Clearly this would be misleading since it did not take into account aggregators or sources other than publisher sites. As Lisa Hinchliffe noted, such a red No Access label actually means "there is no entitled access that is known to exist for all users at this institution on the publisher platform" rather than no access per se.[20] There has been discussion that GetFTR might be moving away from the idea of showing No Access labels and only show links for available items, but as of this writing in March 2022, it is still unclear how this will turn out.

Another hot-button issue is how or whether the GetFTR feature would appear alongside existing delivery mechanisms like link resolvers. The answers to this question might eventually differ depending on the platform.

Ultimately, though, librarians feel uneasy that GetFTR is a way for publishers to create their own alternative to library link resolvers and suspicious that this is a way to control where users end up and take away the choice from users and libraries.

Chris Bulock, an electronic resource librarian at California State University, reviews the appropriate copy problem and compares library link resolvers and GetFTR. Bulock is of the view that "it [is] clear that the intent of GetFTR is not to connect researchers with the most appropriate copy for their needs, but to improve linking through channels that participating publishers control."[21]

From the point of view of many librarians, GetFTR, which is an API, should arguably be just part of the tool kit of linking techniques from which the link resolvers can choose rather than a separate independent one. GetFTR's response so far has been noncommittal. In the FAQ on whether GetFTR works with library link resolvers, the response is "No, not yet," though this use case is being explored.[22]

Finally, in terms of privacy, GetFTR claims that beyond DOIs and affiliations, "it does not require or capture any other information about the user," which is comforting.[23] Still, compared to traditional link resolvers in which the publisher isn't much involved, a move toward GetFTR over traditional link resolvers will make publishers a bigger part of the workflow, which might eventually lead to privacy issues. There's also a tiny caveat to the statement that GetFTR doesn't capture any information about the user, as "integrators can also share user's [sic] IP addresses with GetFTR, although this is optional. Those that choose to share user's [sic] IP addresses with GetFTR and participating publishers have to notify users via their privacy policy ahead of doing so."[24]

Conclusion

Both SeamlessAccess and GetFTR, simply by the virtue of being heavily supported by major journal publishers, have the potential to completely change the way our users get access to resources and journal full text if they choose to adopt these systems on their platforms. At this point, though, both projects are still fairly early in their implementation, and it is unclear how things will pan out. Both projects have of course included other stakeholders, such as librarians and researchers, in the discussion, and it is important for librarians to engage with the issues.

Notes

1. SeamlessAccess, "Privacy, Attributes, and Why They're Important," YouTube video, 8:15, June 8, 2020, https://www.youtube.com/watch?v=4xRqdc0DeJI.
2. IOPscience reported only 3 percent of all usage was via federated access. (OpenAthens, "How IOP Publishing Simplified User Access to IOPscience," YouTube video, 56:26, July 20, 2021, https://www.youtube.com/watch?v=khMp9t0hkZ8.)
3. RA21: Resource Access for the 21st Century, "RA21 Position Statement on Access Brokers," August 23,

2018, https://ra21.org/what-is-ra21/ra21-position-statement-on-access-brokers/.

4. NISO, *Recommended Practices for Improved Access to Institutionally-Provided Information Resources: Results from the Resource Access in the 21st Century (RA21) Project*, recommended practice, NISO RP-27-2019 (Baltimore, MD: National Information Standards Organization, June 21, 2019), https://www.niso.org/publications/rp-27-2019-ra21.

5. SeamlessAccess, "Seamless Access and the User Journey," YouTube video, 2:39, August 10, 2021, https://www.youtube.com/watch?v=V5xfPyaIMyI.

6. OpenAthens, "How IOP Publishing Simplified."

7. "REFEDS Community Announces Publication of New Entity Categories," REFEDS, April 6, 2021, https://refeds.org/a/2558.

8. This has led some libraries to run their own identity providers via OpenAthens service.

9. This is not a theoretical issue. Observers such as Lisa Hinchliffe have shown that misconfigurations of SAML have led to exposure of e-mails and personal names. For example, see Lisa Janicke Hinchliffe, "What Will You Do When They Come for Your Proxy Server?," *The Scholarly Kitchen* (blog), January 16, 2018, https://scholarlykitchen.sspnet.org/2018/01/16/what-will-you-do-when-they-come-for-your-proxy-server-ra21/.

10. Dorothea Salo, "Single Sign-on, the Library, and Patron Privacy," presentation slides, November 1, 2021, https://speakerdeck.com/dsalo/single-sign-on-the-library-and-patron-privacy.

11. "Stakeholders > Service Providers," SeamlessAccess, https://seamlessaccess.org/stakeholders/for-service-providers/.

12. Todd A. Carpenter, "Myth Busting: Five Commonly Held Misconceptions about RA21 (and One Rumor Confirmed)," *Scholarly Kitchen* (blog), February 7, 2018, https://scholarlykitchen.sspnet.org/2018/02/07/myth-busting-five-commonly-held-misconceptions-ra21/.

13. Roger C. Schonfeld, "Publishers Announce a Major New Service to Plug Leakage," *Scholarly Kitchen* (blog), December 3, 2019, https://scholarlykitchen.sspnet.org/2019/12/03/publishers-announce-plug-leakage/.

14. "GetFTR: Dataflows and User Privacy," GetFTR, November 19, 2021, https://www.getfulltextresearch.com/community/getftr-dataflows-and-user-privacy/.

15. GetFTR also offers "Deferred Authentication (federated authentication provided by publisher)," where the user authenticates only after clicking on the first GetFTR link, as well as authentication before or after a search. ("Usability Guidelines," GetFTR, March 2020, https://www.getfulltextresearch.com/for-integrators/usability-guidelines/.)

16. Cindi Trainor and Jason Price, *Rethinking Library Linking: Breathing New Life into OpenURL* (Chicago: American Library Association, 2010).

17. NISO, *KBART Automation: Automated Retrieval of Customer Electronic Holdings*, recommended practice, NISO RP-26-2019 (Baltimore, MD: National Information Standards Organization, June 18, 2019), http://www.niso.org/publications/rp-26-2019-kbartautomation.

18. Lisa Janicke Hinchliffe, "Why Are Librarians Concerned about GetFTR?" *Scholarly Kitchen* (blog), December 10, 2019, https://scholarlykitchen.sspnet.org/2019/12/10/why-are-librarians-concerned-about-getftr/.

19. "Updating the Community," GetFTR, accessed November 19, 2021, https://www.getfulltextresearch.com/community/updating-the-community/.

20. Hinchliffe, "Why Are Librarians Concerned?"

21. Chris Bulock, "Get Full Text Research and the Search for Appropriate Copies," *Serials Review* 46, no. 2 (2020): 160–62, https://doi.org/10.1080/00987913.2020.1759361.

22. "Why GetFTR and FAQs," GetFTR, accessed November 19, 2021, https://www.getfulltextresearch.com/why-use-getftr/.

23. "GetFTR: Dataflows and User Privacy."

24. "GetFTR: Dataflows and User Privacy."

Chapter 5

Other Delivery Solutions

Google's Campus Activated Subscriber Access (CASA) and Entitlement Checks in Content Syndication Partnerships with ResearchGate

Introduction

In chapter 3, we covered the access broker browser extensions adopted by many academic libraries to help their users overcome the many difficulties caused by less-than-user-friendly authentication and authorization methods. In chapter 4, we covered the efforts of publisher-backed projects SeamlessAccess and Get-FTR to tackle these issues at the source by creating new protocols and methods to solve some of them. However, these are not the only solutions. In this chapter, we will cover Google-backed Campus Activated Subscriber Access (CASA) as well as developments in entitlement checks for content syndication with ResearchGate.

What Is Campus Activated Subscriber Access (CASA)?

Campus Activated Subscriber Access (CASA) was introduced by Google in 2017 and has quickly become supported by an impressive list of content owners, including publishers and aggregators—HeinOnline, Gale, JSTOR, Ingenta Connect, HighWire-hosted journals, Wiley, Project Muse, APA, EBSCOhost, Emerald, Springer Nature, Elsevier, and more.

This list of content owners that support this standard—comparable to the current list of supporters of RA21/SeamlessAccess or GetFTR—has mostly flown under the radar in the eyes of many users and librarians. This is probably because some content owners have automatically turned on this feature (opting

users in by default), coupled with the fact that, when this feature works, it automatically and seamlessly grants access to users who may not even notice what is happening. So what does CASA do?

Recall that in chapter 1 we talked about the problems of IP recognition when users are off campus. Because they are off campus, they do not have the right IP range and can't be easily recognized as users from an institution that is entitled to access the resource.

This situation led to solutions such as proxies and browser extensions, which are often inconvenient (as described in chapters 2 and 3). SAML-based methods, which are improved by SeamlessAccess (chapter 4), promise to make consistent, intuitive single sign-on a reality, but for them to work, both institutions and content owners need to support SAML and be in the same identity federation. This leads to a question: Is there a way to enable users to experience single sign-on without relying on SAML?

CASA's solution is for the user's browser to remember and record their affiliation from when they were either on campus or using a proxy (so they can benefit from IP authentication), such that when they are off campus and not using a proxy, they can still benefit from those earlier recorded affiliations.

In practice, CASA leverages the fact that Google Scholar, unlike the library home page, may be one of the most popular starting points for an academic search. As CASA is an extension of the Google Scholar Subscriber Links program, you need to understand what Subscriber Links are. Unlike Library Links, where Google Scholar gets holdings information from

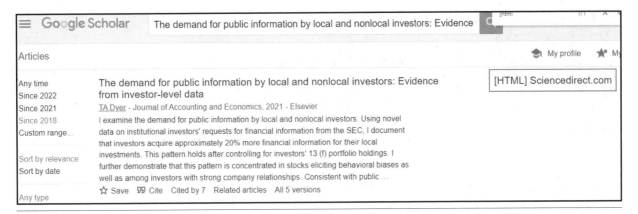

Figure 5.1
Example of a Subscriber Link

the library, Subscriber Links depend on entitlement and subscription data from the publishers. When users see search results in Google Scholar—assuming they are on campus with the right IP address and the articles are from participating content owners—they may see some links on the right side of the search results that, when clicked, give them access to the full-text resources. These links are called Subscriber Links. See figure 5.1 for an example of a Subscriber Link. Note: This Subscriber Link can coexist with links added by Library Links if it applies.

In the background, the following is occurring:

1. A user lands on a page of results in Google Scholar.
2. Google Scholar looks up the list of subscriptions accessible to the user (based on IP address) from the Subscriber Links data it received from content owners.
3. Based on the data found, Subscriber Links (access links to the subscribed articles) appear in the Google Scholar interface for on-campus users.

CASA comes into play when this subscription data for each user based on affiliation is stored as a token in a cookie (see figure 5.2).

The magic happens when the user using the same browser with the CASA cookie is now off campus. If they try the same search on Google Scholar, those subscription links will appear again. More importantly, when the user clicks on these links, they will be sent to the publisher site. But instead of not having access because they are off campus, the publisher will use the CASA cookie to allow access (see figure 5.3).

As noted on Google Scholar's help page, in such a situation this will "indicate your subscription access to participating publishers so that they can allow you to read the full-text of these articles without logging in or using a proxy."[1] This recording is done via the stored cookie. But you might say this is useful only if the off-campus user is trying to access journal articles

from Google Scholar. But what happens if the user is not trying to access the resource from Google Scholar? This is where a variant known as Universal CASA comes into play.

If you have a CASA cookie and visit publishers that support this feature, you will see on the right of each article a small gray badge with the label PDF or HTML that allows access when you click on it. Google calls such links "off-campus access links." See figure 5.4 for an example.

An early adopter of CASA noted that you don't need a Google account to benefit from CASA, but if you created the CASA cookie while logged into your Google account, other devices logged on with the same account will benefit from CASA cookies.[2] There is one catch to CASA. This benefit normally lasts for thirty days only. In other words, to benefit from CASA, you need to be on campus (or otherwise authenticate via IP) every thirty days. As of this writing, this time period has increased to 120 days in response to the fact that users may now work remotely more due to COVID-19. Users who do not trust Google (particularly if the Universal CASA feature will share data with Google) and do not want to use this feature can go into the Google Scholar settings, click on Account, and uncheck "Signed-in off campus access links."

CASA Compared

Google CASA at its best is free to use and truly seamless, as there is no need to sign in at all as long as you have a valid CASA cookie. Unlike SeamlessAccess, it also does not require the institution to invest in configurations for federated SAML access. It also partners with a wide range of content owners, including aggregators such as EBSCOhost, which solutions like GetFTR do not yet cover. One unique selling point of CASA is that this solution, once enabled, can work on multiple devices, including mobile devices, at the

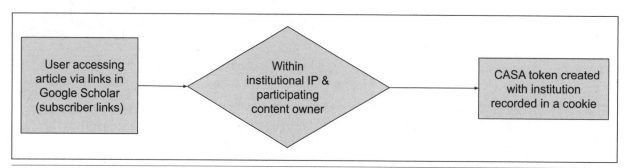

Figure 5.2
Process of creating a CASA cookie

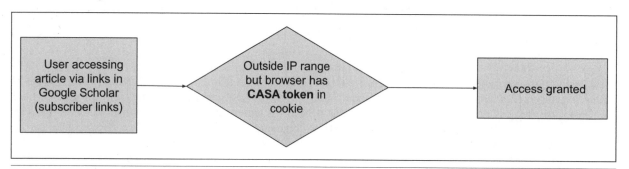

Figure 5.3
Process of granting access based on CASA cookie

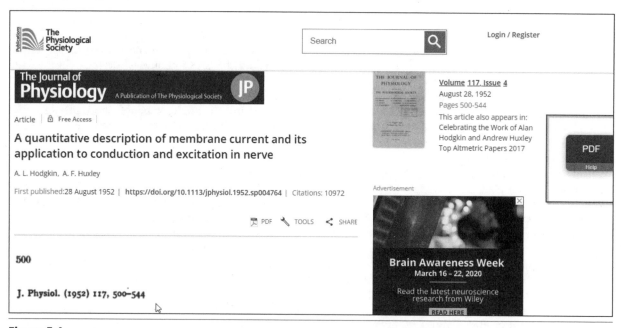

Figure 5.4
Example of a Universal CASA access link appearing when not accessing via Google Scholar

same time if you sync the CASA cookie with your Google account.

There are a couple of drawbacks. First, as already mentioned, to benefit fully from this solution such that it works across all your devices, you need to associate it with your Google account, which means giving up even more of your privacy to Google. Second,

you need to remember to continually validate your CASA cookie every thirty days (currently 120 days due to the COVID situation). CASA is built on top of the Subscriber Links program. It is important to note the subscription or entitlement data on what the user can access comes from the content owner, not the library. This makes it similar to GetFTR, which, as discussed in chapter 4, is both advantageous and disadvantageous.

Lastly, while there have been privacy concerns that access broker browser extensions and SAML assertations could identify the user, CASA might have even more privacy implications given that Google itself is able to associate and track your research activity even if you are not signed into your Google account at all.

ResearchGate and Content Syndication

ResearchGate is probably the largest academic social network, or scholarly collaboration network, reaching millions of researchers. However, it has been controversial for many reasons, but mainly because it has been accused of illegally hosting millions of papers that infringe on publishers' copyrights.

This issue came to a head when the Coalition for Responsible Sharing, consisting of publishers such as ACS and Elsevier, was formed in 2017 to take "formal steps to address the illicit dissemination of enormous amounts of published journal articles on Research-Gate's website."[3] Some members of this organization, including ACS and Elsevier, have even taken legal action in the US and Germany.[4] However, other publishers, including Springer Nature, Cambridge University Press, and Thieme, have instead managed to come to agreements with ResearchGate on how to manage sharing of their content.[5] A few publishers, notably Springer Nature, Wiley, Hindawi, and Rockefeller University Press, have also started content syndication pilots with ResearchGate. But what is content syndication?

What Is Content Syndication?

In the journal publishing business, there have generally been two models under which an institution could gain and provide access for its users.

Institutions could subscribe to a journal directly from the publisher, such as Wiley or Sage. Alternatively, they could subscribe to an aggregator that serves as an intermediate distributor of content. The aggregator licenses the content from the publisher and resells it to institutions that sign a contract with the aggregator. The key thing to note is that the aggregator hosts the subscribed content on its own aggregator platform (which is different from the publisher platform) so users whose institutions provide access only via the aggregator will be able to access the content only via the aggregator platform and not via the publisher sites. This can be frustrating to users if they land on the publisher sites via methods such as Google (which is a common occurrence) and are unable to gain access.

In a content syndication model, institutions continue to subscribe to content from publishers. However,

publishers can "put their content in the discovery and access pathways that users have adopted. Users who are entitled to access the materials, based on an existing license typically between the publisher and the library, would be able to do so on almost any site."[6]

In this case, publishers such as Springer Nature and Wiley have signed content syndication agreements that allow ResearchGate to carry full-text version-of-record papers on the platform for selected journals. This benefits users because a growing number of users spend a lot of time on ResearchGate. In return, ResearchGate shares usage data with publishers on the success of these arrangements, possibly via the Distributed Usage Logging System, which was first supported by COUNTER Code of Practice—Release 5.[7] For example, Wiley's first content syndication pilot with ResearchGate included eighteen open-access gold journals and seventy-eight hybrid journals.[8]

Authentication and Authorization on ResearchGate

An interesting question is how ResearchGate will handle access of articles syndicated on its platform. While Springer Nature's first iteration of its content syndication deal did not enforce any access controls at all, later versions started to do so. Currently it is unclear how ResearchGate implements access controls except it does not appear to be supporting SAML-based methods. Early tests by Lisa Hinchliffe and Roger Schonfeld suggest that ResearchGate is using some combination of IP address and ResearchGate profile.[9] This is also mentioned by Wiley.[10] Since ResearchGate profiles currently aren't verified, it's likely these checks aren't 100 percent reliable, but this area will no doubt see further experiment and refinement for entitlement checks.

Conclusion

In this chapter, we covered two other authentication and authorization methods—namely, Google's Campus Activated Subscriber Access (CASA) and entitlement checks based on IP and ResearchGate profiles in content syndication partnerships between publishers and ResearchGate. This completes our coverage of the major authentication and authorization techniques in use currently. In the final chapter we will conclude with an overall summary and some thoughts on the future.

Notes

1. "Access to Articles," in "Search Tips," Google Scholar help, accessed November 24, 2021, https://scholar .google.com/intl/en/scholar/help.html#access. See also Elsevier, "What Is Google CASA?," ScienceDirect

Support Center, accessed February 28, 2022, https://service.elsevier.com/app/answers/detail/a_id/29795/supporthub/sciencedirect/.

2. "Campus Activated Subscriber Access (CASA)," High-Wire Press, accessed November 24, 2021, https://www.highwirepress.com/resources/data-sheets/casa-faq/.

3. "The Coalition for Responsible Sharing and Research-Gate," Coalition for Responsible Sharing, accessed November 26, 2021, http://www.responsiblesharing.org/about-us/background/.

4. "ACS and Elsevier Ask US Courts to Address ResearchGate's Copyright Responsibility," Coalition for Responsible Sharing, October 3, 2018, http://www.responsiblesharing.org/2018-10-03-acs-and-elsevier-ask-us-courts-to-address-researchgates-copyright-responsibility/.

5. ResearchGate, "Springer Nature, Cambridge University Press, Thieme and ResearchGate Announce New Cooperation to Make It Easier to Navigate the Legal Sharing of Academic Journal Articles," news release, April 19, 2018, https://www.researchgate.net/blog/post/springer-nature-cambridge-university-press-thieme-and-researchgate-announce-new-cooperation-to-make-it-easier-to-navigate-the-legal-sharing-of-academic-journal-articles.

6. Roger C. Schonfeld, "What Is Content Syndication?" *Ithaka S+R* (blog), March 1, 2019, https://sr.ithaka.org/blog/what-is-content-syndication/.

7. Roger C. Schonfeld, "Will Publishers Syndicate Their Content?" *Scholarly Kitchen* (blog), October 15, 2018, https://scholarlykitchen.sspnet.org/2018/10/15/syndicate-content/.

8. "Easily Access Wiley Research, Directly on ResearchGate," Wiley Online Library, accessed November 26, 2021, https://onlinelibrary.wiley.com/researchers/read/find-research/wiley-researchgate-pilot.

9. Lisa Janicke Hinchliffe and Roger C. Schonfeld, "Diverting Leakage to the Library Subscription Channel," *Scholarly Kitchen* (blog), July 16, 2019, https://scholarlykitchen.sspnet.org/2019/07/16/diverting-leakage-to-subscription/.

10. "Easily Access Wiley Research."

Chapter 6

Improving Access to and Delivery of Academic Content from Libraries

A Roundup

Introduction

In the prior five chapters, we have gone through a whirlwind of tools, protocols, and standards related to authentication and authorization, including IP recognition, SAML-based methods, access broker browser extensions, SeamlessAccess, GetFTR, and Campus Activated Subscriber Access (CASA).

As many of these developments are still new, academic libraries will need to be on their toes to keep abreast of these coming changes. In this concluding chapter, I will provide some practical advice on how to do so.

Some Practical Steps: Taking the Bird's-Eye View

How and what your institution should support is very much a function of your user community's interests, context, and resources.

You might already be supporting some of these delivery methods: for example, promoting the use of an access broker browser extension or having varying degrees of support for SAML federated access. While it may be tempting to work on each of these developments separately—for example, forming a project team to evaluate and select a suitable access broker browser extension or forming yet another project team to study implementation and support of SeamlessAccess and GetFTR—this can lead to piecemeal efforts that fail to see the whole picture.

Instead, I suggest that a better approach (particularly if it has never been done before) is to form a cross-functional team of library staff members across various departments (liaison librarians, library IT, and electronic resource librarians) to conduct an audit to see where the library stands in terms of support for each of the methods covered in the earlier chapters.

It is also important to bring in the voice of the customer whenever possible, and faculty, students, campus IT, and other stakeholders should be brought in when necessary to ensure a complete picture. Some questions to consider for this task force:

- Do our users consider delivery a big issue? What situations or scenarios are the biggest pain points?
- What options to improve delivery are currently available for our users, and how aware are users of these options?
- What do our stakeholders, both librarians and users, think about the tradeoff between convenience and risk of loss of privacy?
- Do we have the in-house technical expertise to evaluate the issues (e.g., privacy risks of SeamlessAccess, GetFTR, and access broker browser extensions)? If not, how should we build expertise?

Some Long-Term Scenarios

Currently, developments in this area of librarianship are still in flux, and there are many uncertainties about how things will turn out. Nobody has a crystal ball; however, it might be instructive to consider the following three scenarios to trigger discussion for your planning. These scenarios attempt to forecast a

Library Technology Reports   alatechsource.org   August/September 2022

future in 2027 to 2032, five to ten years after the publication of this report.

Scenario One: SeamlessAccess and GetFTR Become Widely Adopted

In this scenario, the publisher-backed SeamlessAccess and GetFTR have become widely supported by most journal publishers and platforms alike. IP authentication for library resources has become a rarity as institutions and content owners are mostly supporting SAML federated access. Most users have long become customized to clicking on the "Log in via Your Institution" button to benefit from SeamlessAccess, and when they encounter the rare resource that requires IP authentication and proxies, they are extremely dissatisfied.

While privacy leaks via SAML entity attributes still occasionally occur, standards have been put in place, and most institutions are careful enough to avoid such issues. Meanwhile, GetFTR has finally solved the technical and coordination issues of getting aggregators on board as content providers, and major aggregators such as EBSCO and ProQuest are now supported. As a result, most scholarly platforms now support GetFTR. Platforms that do not have the technical capability to implement GetFTR opt for supporting LibKey linking or Google CASA, while the most sophisticated platforms, such as Semantic Scholar, support both.

While use of library link resolvers has declined somewhat, they continue to still be used because GetFTR supports only DOI resolvable content, and in any case Google Scholar has stubbornly refused to support GetFTR. Access broker browser extensions have declined in popularity due to the combined effects of SeamlessAccess and GetFTR reducing the need for such extensions. Some of these browser extensions instead pivoted to support discovery and recommendations and helped to bring librarians into the user's workflow.

This is an optimistic scenario for the future, of course.

Scenario Two: A Hybrid Future

This is the status quo scenario. While SeamlessAccess and GetFTR continued to make strides in development, they ultimately did not become a complete universal solution.

In the case of SeamlessAccess, there were a couple of barriers. First, while major publishers were capable of making the technical investment to support SeamlessAccess and the underlying federated access method, this still left out hundreds of smaller publishers and content owners that did not have the capability. Similarly, while many institutions were capable of supporting federated access methods, with libraries either running their own IdPs via OpenAthens or relying on campus IT, many institutions were not. Some chose not to, due to privacy concerns. As a result, most publishers still maintain support for IP authentication and proxies, and ultimately SeamlessAccess did not achieve its aim of displacing IP authentication. Similarly, GetFTR, while it is commonly seen on many platforms such as Mendeley and Scopus, ultimately cannot be a complete solution as it has not managed to solve the technical issues regarding supporting aggregators. As a result, access broker browser extensions remain popular, and users live in a fragmented ecosystem where SeamlessAccess and GetFTR are just two of many options.

This scenario seems to me personally to be the most likely future with the landscape of access management becoming a hybrid one.

Scenario Three: Open Access Triumphant

In this scenario, developments in scholarly communications have led to the much-anticipated open-access world. Whether it is Plan S or Subscribe to Open (S2O)[1] or some other business model, someone finally cracked the code, and most journal content (say, more than 90 percent) is born open access for version of record.

As noted in the last section of chapter 1, this does not totally remove the need for authentication and authorization, as many licensed library resources—such as abstracting and indexing, financial, and other non-open-access databases—continue to require access management. Still, in this future, we see a decline in the importance of such technologies, even though publishers try to encourage single sign-ons via SeamlessAccess even when a user is accessing open-access content.

While I believe we certainly will have made substantial progress in open access by 2032, it seems unlikely to me that the vast majority of new publications will be automatically open access. In my personal opinion, this is the least likely of the three scenarios. Of course, if this scenario does come to pass, I believe it will result in a substantial rethink of academic librarianship beyond the impact on access management of resources.

Other Scenarios

These are just three straightforward projections of the future of libraries in delivery, and other scenarios exist. As they say, the best way to predict the future is to make it, so hopefully this exercise in scenario planning will allow you to not just plan for your institution but also advocate for the future together with others.

Resources to Keep Abreast of Developments

- GetFTR official website—https://www.getfulltext research.com
- SeamlessAccess official website—https://seamless access.org
- Comparison of access broker browser extensions (regularly updated)—http://musingsaboutlibrari anship.blogspot.com/2019/07/a-comparison-of -6-access-broker-browser.html

Conclusion

While providing access to needed resources may not be as exciting or glamorous as providing users support in discovery, information literacy instruction, and research support in digital scholarship, a core part of our library service is to provide users with access to the resources they need.

Even with the rise of open access, I believe providing more seamless and reliable access to resources remains one of the most critical tasks of libraries. I hope this report has given you food for thought on the various ways libraries can provide such support and some clarity on how this area might change in the coming years.

Note

1. For more information on these models, visit https://www.coalition-s.org and https://subscribetoopencom munity.org.

Library Technology
REPORTS

Upcoming Issues	
October 58:7	**The Current Landscape of Electronic Resources Access Issues** by Ashley Zmau and Holly Talbott
Nov/Dec 58:8	**Bibliometrics Tools and Technologies in Academia** by Laura Bredahl

Purchase single copies in the ALA Store
alastore.ala.org

ALA TechSource

alatechsource.org

ALA TechSource, a unit of the publishing department of the American Library Association

A Note to Our Subscribers

As a subscription-based publication, *Library Technology Reports* will sunset with the December 2022 issue. After that time, it will be available for single-issue sales only. Subsequently, no new *Library Technology Reports* subscriptions or renewals will be accepted. If you have questions about your subscription, please contact us at subscriptions@ala.org or call toll free at (800) 545-2433, ext. 4299.